THE FORBIDDEN BOOK

William Tyndale and the First English Bible

Photos of *Foxe's Book of Martyrs* taken by:
Daystar Studio, Shippensburg, PA

Lollard House

a division of
Destiny Image Publishers, Inc.®
P.O. Box 310
Shippensburg, PA 17257-0310

ISBN 1-56043-950-5

For Worldwide Distribution
Printed in the U.S.A.

Third Printing: 1993   Fourth Printing: 1995

Destiny Image books are available through these fine distributors outside the United States:

Christian Growth, Inc.
Jalan Kilang-Timor, Singapore 0315

Vine Christian Centre
Mid Glamorgan, Wales, United Kingdom

Rhema Ministries Trading
Randburg, South Africa

Vision Resources
Ponsonby, Auckland, New Zealand

Salvation Book Centre
Petaling, Jaya, Malaysia

WA Buchanan Company
Geebung, Queensland, Australia

Successful Christian Living
Capetown, Rep. of South Africa

Word Alive
Niverville, Manitoba, Canada

Inside the U.S., call toll free to order:
1-800-722-6774

Contents

Dedication

To
the Living Word
who is not limited
to a written language.

Prologue

With its thousands of gods in the first century, the Roman state was satan's refinement of control over God's people and His creation. Religion was pure mysticism. Monotheism was the mother and twin sister of despair, evidenced by a Jewish people downtrodden and divided. The shekinah glory of Israel had departed, the ten northern tribes of David's united kingdom had been dispersed seven hundred years previously, and most Jews from the captivity in Babylon (500 B.C.) had refused to return to their homeland. Civil unrest in Palestine was rampant and the "nation" was ruled by Herod, a demoniac. All roads led to Rome and hopelessness characterized the nations under Rome's dominion. Britain was the "uttermost part" of the earth and a thorn in the side of

Rome, possessing the only people to face the Roman legions and fight them to a standstill. The Britons were an unusual people with an unusual destiny.

How many people today realize that Constantine was a Briton? All records prove that fact, but history was rewritten to favor a different origin and authority for the Christian Church. For by his assuming the title of Roman Caesar, Rome became the seat of the Christian Church and the origin of Christianity had to be rewritten in order to validate its authority. But when Pope Gregory sent Augustine to "Christianize" England in A.D. 590, two hundred seventy-five years after Constantine, Augustine faithfully recorded the existence of Christianity in England many centuries before his arrival.

It is in Glastonbury, England, tradition teaches, that the mother church for English Christianity was founded and nurtured by Joseph of Arimethea in approximately A.D. 36, just three years after the death and resurrection of Jesus. This new Christian religion overwhelmed Druidism, spreading to Wales, Cornwall, Scotland and Ireland. It solidified a people destined to face the Roman legions in a siege that lasted for three hundred years.

It took the person of God in the flesh (the Incarnation) to de-mystify Rome and break satan's dominion on earth. Jesus did so through obedience, not through the passive resistance of Gandhi. Man's "obedience to God" is "resistance to tyranny" in the Judeo-Christian world, but secular historians are ever careful to reject the spiritual elements so plainly evident in world history. In fact, every modern history book is "his" or "her" story as contrasted to the Christian and Jew who view history as "His" story.

The Word of God is the record of God's control over history. The books of that record are filled with man's hope of Heaven through courage and endurance and their acting on the hundreds of promises God honors for those who trust Him. The Bible is not the on-going quest for man to find God, but the story of God leaving Heaven and seeking out man.

Jesus Christ was a revolutionary who confounded His antagonists. Caesar was considered a deity, with all the powers of that position. The Roman Empire was satan's masterpiece, a finely-tuned apparatus rebuilt on his failures in Babylon, Assyria, Persia and Greece. It took less than five seconds for Jesus to strip Caesar of his deity: "Render unto Caesar that which is Caesar's and unto God that which is God's" (Matt. 22:21). In the process, Caesar became just another king and God was forever restored to His eternal position.

A thousand years of satan's fine-tuning to gain control of the earth was destroyed in the length of time it took for Jesus Christ to proclaim those fourteen words. The modern church rarely teaches the truth of His accomplishment, thereby fueling the fires of tyranny that every government seeks and allowing governments—even that of the United States—to become the instrument of Antichrist. The Antichrist will give the impression of a "substitute deliverer," which is the word's definition. Eventually a one-world government run by man to secure peace will cause men to follow after it and, in the process, forsake Christ and His teaching.

Jesus Christ was the "Lamb of God, the adequate sacrifice to take away the sins of the world" (John 1:29). That accomplishment (promise) was fulfilled when He became obedient to His death on the cross. With His death and burial, the law was satisfied; with His resurrection, man was justified—because He lives! His last words (the Great Commission) before His ascendancy contained His promises to "come again" and to strive with man until the end of the world. These promises are given to those who "Go ye therefore and teach all nations..." (Matt. 28:19).

The fruit of Joseph of Arimethea's work in the island nation of England led to the west coast of Scotland where lies the little island of Iona, only 2.5 miles long and 1.5 miles wide, with but a few hundred acres of arable land. There in 564, during the "Christianizing" of Europe, a missionary from Ireland named Columba established a school of prophets. For thirty-four years they trained and evangelized the mainland and neighboring islands.

The college at Iona was hardly a monastery—the faculty were allowed to marry and the curriculum was designed to train Christian scholars and missionaries to go forth as soldiers of Christ, conquering and occupying the outlying territories of heathenism. This little island housed a school that did more to carry a pure gospel to all parts of Britain and Europe during the Dark Ages (A.D. 500-800) than all of Christendom combined.

The scholars and students from Iona were called "Culdees." They declared the authority of Scripture and called for the establishment of elders (presbyters) in each church for governing; they claimed their origin from the apostles John and Paul. This doctrine was in conflict with Roman Christianity and eventually they would violently collide.

The Culdee Church was driven underground in 1297 as the Roman Church suppressed the centers of learning and dispersed the teachers. These teachers continued their work in remote parts of Scotland and beyond; however, after 1297 the old Culdee Church disappeared as a visible organization.

As the ancient faith moved underground, its inheritors continued to promote reform. These Reformers were in every country before the Reformation. Persecution kept the movement hidden; nevertheless, throughout Scotland were found small assemblies who looked to Jesus Christ as the only mediator between God and man. In England, John Wycliffe was a product of the Culdee doctrine, and his followers became known by the name that we recognize today as Lollards. In 1494 thirty persons called

"The Lollards of Kyle" (near Glasgow) were brought before the Archbishop on a heresy charge. That heresy proved to be their practicing the ancient Culdee Church doctrines.

Satan's death-grip on England in Wycliffe's day and during the fourteen decades leading up to the Reformation was reminiscent of his grip on Rome. The devil had denied the people God's Word and possessed the Church with the notion that it would be better to obey the pope's laws than God's.

God found John Wycliffe and John Huss in the fourteenth century, John Colet and Jerome Savonarola in the fifteenth, and William Tyndale and Martin Luther in the sixteenth century just like He found the apostle Paul in the first. God uses men who trust and obey Him to restore men to His ways.

God conducted His orchestra of saints and prepared, or shaped, the battlefield for the coming war. Obediently Wycliffe translated and trained; obediently the Lollards (Wycliffe's students) practiced his teaching, becoming the instrument for distributing God's Word and providing a selection of young "Pauls" to act when the hour for decision came. Their courage and endurance was truly remarkable. Looking to the end of the fifteenth century, one hundred fifteen years after Wycliffe's death, circumstantial evidence leads to John Colet as the secret leader of the Lollards and direct evidence persuades us that the Lollards secretly marked many of the Reformers (often without those Reformers' knowledge) to accomplish the hidden agenda of making God's Word accessible to the nations. We know that Colet financed Erasmus, influenced Tyndale and was personally responsible for letting Paul "speak." A similar circumstance was experienced by Staupitz, the benefactor of Luther, who realized that the qualities Luther possessed were necessary to lead in Germany. It was Staupitz who gave Luther his first Bible and encouraged him to preach in public.

Many of those of influence are lost to us today and will never be known. Like those in Damascus, who let Paul over the wall by holding the ropes (Acts 9:25), their names are known only to God; nevertheless, they share the eternal rewards of the apostle and the Reformers for their obedience and sacrifice.

The apostle Paul's last earthly request, preserved in Second Timothy 4, was for Timothy to bring him the books and parchments. The year was A.D. 66. Paul's last written words were designed to solidify the record for those who would come later. The cornerstone for the churches Paul established was that "All Scripture is given by inspiration of God" (II Tim. 3:16).

For thirty-three years following the Resurrection the Holy Spirit chose men as His instruments to write the letters and books that comprise the New Testament. These writings ceased by the end of the first century and became the standard for Christians wherever the gospel was taught. The message would be translated into Latin, Armenian, Syriac, Coptic and all languages of the recipients of the gospel for five hundred years.

The Hebrew law translated to Greek, the Septuagint (LXX), was recognized as the canon of the Old Testament. In A.D. 397, the Synod of Carthage officially declared twenty-seven books of the New Testament era to be accepted as Scripture and the LXX to be accepted as Old Testament Scripture with a footnote on the fourteen Apocryphal books to be included for instruction and history, but not as Holy Writ.

In Bethlehem, Jerome, the most outstanding linguist and scholar of his age, had been commissioned by Pope Damasus to translate those works from Greek manuscripts in his possession. In time (500 years) the western Church would universally accept the Latin Vulgate. But as the centuries passed in the West, the Latin Vulgate was corrupted by unfaithful copying and the interpretation of the canon was restricted to a few dozen scholars in each generation who usurped the Holy Spirit's ability to act through individual instruction, for which the Word of God was intended.

Such was the state of affairs in Wycliffe's day in 1380, Erasmus' day in 1516 and Tyndale's in 1525.

Preface

It was the darkest of times. "Religion" and superstition ruled and broke the backs of the masses in Europe and England. But from time to time, in this spiritual and moral vacuum, a few voices of hope could be heard.

For example, in 1417 John Oldcastle tried to overthrow the tyranny of the Church of England. But the effort was squelched, with great suffering. Posthumously, John Wycliffe became the most admired scholar and preacher in England. The admiration of the people and his fame held the criticism of the Church at bay, but in time, his teaching was driven underground.

It was William Tyndale and his English translation of the Bible that finally cracked the walls of spiritual tyranny in that land. In fact, Tyndale's translation of the Bible not only changed the course of English history, it also altered the spread of the gospel worldwide. What was it in Tyndale's life and work that so profoundly affected the course of history? Can we see patterns that need to be recalled and repeated in our times?

The Forbidden Book attempts to recapture the spirit of William Tyndale. Tyndale's love for the Lord and for the Word of God focused his mind, concentration and energies and drove him to produce the English Bible for the people. If there is to be reformation for Christ today in our culture, there are certain "Tyndale" characteristics we may need to recover.

First, we need ability. Tyndale was a gifted linguist. He was skilled in Hebrew, Greek, Latin, Italian, Spanish, English, French and German. Tyndale clearly understood the thought patterns of his world. But he concentrated on translating the Greek and Hebrew into noble and articulate English.

Second, we need purity of study. Tyndale repudiated the "religious" education of his day. He abandoned the pursuit of a degree in divinity for direct study and exposition of God's Word, apart from scholastic interpretation.

Third, we need purpose. Tyndale felt strongly that the Bible should be in the hands of the people and in their own tongue so they could escape the depths of churchly superstition, ignorance and abuse.

Fourth, we need commitment. Tyndale stayed virtually with one task until his death. He could not be dissuaded or distracted. Although he sought counsel, advice and teaching from friends and others such as Luther, he walked alone with the Holy Spirit in carrying forth his God-given purpose.

In order for reformation and revival to occur today, God must raise up schools and churches, teachers and pastors who burn with zeal and who sell out to the truth like William Tyndale. Tyndale has set the example. We must know our callings and purposes in life and refuse to deviate.

To again understand the heart of the Reformation, students of the Word need to study Wycliffe, Tyndale, Luther, Calvin and others. Those same students need to fervently study God's Word as these great men of the past did. Then they can speak to our generation with the razor sharpness of truth and with a deep flowing understanding of what Moses, David, Paul and Peter wrote under the inspiration of the Spirit of God.

This first American writing of a study of Tyndale, *The Forbidden Book*, tells of all the elements that composed the makeup of a William Tyndale. In noble words, Chapter 5 of the book sums up the purposes of this man. May the same be found today in young men and women who give their lives sacrificially in the service of Christ. William Tyndale was a martyr. He was but one in "the sea of martyrs whose sacrifice broke the chains and let God's Word go free..."

Dr. Mal Couch
Tyndale Biblical Institute and Seminary
6800 Brentwood Stair
Ft. Worth, TX 76112
817-446-1415

Photos of woodcuts in this book are taken from *Foxe's Book of Martyrs*.

Introduction

If Martin Luther and William Tyndale had espoused the popular teachings of the twentieth century church, there would have been no Reformation and certainly no modern English state, no commonwealth of free English nations or "free" church under the banner of Protestantism. Although this may be an extreme analysis, in spite of state and church abuses in the sixteenth century there was, for a brief moment, a window of opportunity to circulate the "Forbidden Book" among the peasants and merchants, clergy and royalty, soldiers and criminals—to seize the day and free the masses from beneath their bondage to the Church.

The driving force in Martin Luther's life was the fear of God, while the belief that God had chosen him for his work possessed William Tyndale. Their love and respect for God overcame their personal fears and persuaded them to undertake a work that, from a human perspective, was virtually impossible.

William Tyndale abhorred the conduct of the Church, its corrupt bishops and its begging friars. At an early age God's Word made such an impact on him that he was driven to be a part of the process that would allow the common man to know God directly from His divine revelation. It was inconceivable to William Tyndale that the hierarchy of the Church would resist that proposition if he could but show them how wonderfully the Bible in the English language could reveal God. The ingredients necessary for that task were courage and endurance.

Tyndale would have failed without Luther, and Luther would have failed without Tyndale. Luther knew that the reforms he championed would be short-lived if England as a nation remained neutral to his theology. Furthermore, the yoke of bondage daily administered by the Roman Church would win if the monarch to succeed Henry VIII were to bow his knee to Rome.

The present investigation into the historical events of this era concerns the birth of a gifted child in 1494 named William Tyndale in western England, near Bristol, the nation's second largest city and seaport. The year 1492 is a date in every child's history book in every nation. Christopher Columbus had discovered America. The western world was awakening from a deep sleep of nearly a thousand years. The universities of Paris, Cambridge and Oxford were being radically influenced with the "New Learning," only recently received in Italy, of the Greek language. A new breed of educator had been awakened by the Greek language, which the Church was cautiously tolerating. Besides, the bureaucracy and the enemies of innovation were timid in dealing with educators who held prestigious and powerful positions and who sought to teach the Greek language. Men like Savonarola in Italy and Colet in England could now allow the apostle Paul to speak in the first century language, from the ancient Greek manuscripts, to the people.

Chapter 1

Wycliffe and the Rise of the Lollards

The Roman Church achieved a powerful foothold after the death of Emperor Constantine I in the fourth century. The Holy Roman Empire governed the western world from Constantinople in the east to England in the west and the Germanic states in the north. The Church at Rome maintained control by virtue of strategically placed monasteries that had a monopoly on education, spiritual life and safety throughout the Empire. Each monastery was as strong as its leadership, and freedom to lead was often directly proportional to the distance from Rome. Isolated outbreaks of religious freedom occurred over the centuries, but when discovered, they were suppressed by Rome.

1

For the thousand years that we refer to as the Dark Ages (A.D. 500-800) and the Middle Ages (A.D. 800-1500), the Church at Rome ruled. The technique to sustain its power was simple: Control people's minds by controlling their education, and control their education by controlling their language. One empire, many languages, but only Latin was allowed for education and instruction. Ultimately, the pope's decrees became the textbook of both ecclesiastical and civil law and order. To be fair, there were popes who were tolerant and spiritual, granting freedom of thought, but only in Latin were scholars allowed to communicate. One bad apple can spoil a whole barrel; therefore, one tyrannical pope could undo all the good of his predecessors. The pope was elevated to God's sole agent to lead the Church, and resistance to that leadership was an act of heresy punishable by excommunication, imprisonment or death.

Accumulation of wealth leads to power, and power ultimately provides the mechanism to raise armies to enforce the will of the one in power. Church agents were eventually employed to spy, lie and intimidate in a way that is sadly prescient of Hitler's SS and Stalin's KGB. Such agents of the pope were known as *inquisitors*, and the period that includes our emphasis has been ignominiously referred to as the *Inquisition*. The Inquisition originated in 1233 and metamorphosed in varying degrees throughout the Empire for nearly six hundred years. Resistance to tyranny was driven underground until such time when circumstances permitted the overthrow of the tyrant.

All that is necessary for a tyranny to ascend are successive generations of freedom-loving people who tolerate the tyrants. Consider the words attributed to St. Paul from his triads as recorded in R.W. Morgan's book, *Did The Apostle Paul Visit Britain?*:

1. Obedience to God is resistance to tyranny.

2. There were three sorts of men: The man of God, who renders good for evil; the man of men, who renders good for good and evil for evil; and the man of the devil, who renders evil for good.

Abuses of the Roman Church and its clergy manifested themselves in the spiritual realm of the Church and in the daily existence of the people. The Church demanded auricular confession, penance for pardon, mysticism in the Mass, a belief in the carnal presence of Christ's body in the Sacrament (transubstantiation), pilgrimages and the adoration of saints. It forbade the reading of Scripture books in English or in any language other than Latin.

What forces, pressures, abuses, excesses, distortions and perversions aroused scholars wherever academic freedom was tolerated? What were the circumstances that upset the status quo so that men of letters would risk the security of their position and influence to lash out against the Mother Church which for hundreds of years had dominated people's minds with its sacrosanct grip on peasants and priests, scholars and bishops, princes and kings?

By the first decade of the sixteenth century the list of abuses that mocked truth and made hypocrites of those who remained silent included the following:

1. Over one hundred thousand prostitutes were in the employ of the Church as a universal acceptance of Augustine's proclamation of prostitution as a "necessary evil."

2. "Artifacts belonging to Jesus" were strategically enshrined for the purpose of drawing lay people into undertaking pilgrimages sponsored by the Church at exorbitant prices.

3. Indulgences were granted for crimes that ranged from adultery to murder and rendered the state powerless to prosecute the criminal. (It was well known that Pope Julius (1503-1515) granted such an indulgence to the future Pope Leo X (1515-1521) who was married with two children—so much for priestly celibacy. It was also widely known that Erasmus was the illegitimate son of a priest. Indulgences were often granted for money paid in advance for a criminal act not yet performed.)

4. On the Continent, Bishop Tetzel, the special envoy to both Julius and Leo, extracted enormous sums of money from the parishes for the construction of St. Peter's Basilica by granting pardon for penances in Purgatory.

5. Julius and Leo declared the Holy Wars to justify mass slaughter of the Jews in order to steal their

money and possessions to finance the building of the Vatican, primarily the Sistine Chapel and St. Peter's Basilica. Pope Leo X revealed the truth of his convictions in his utterance, "How profitable the fable of Christ has been to us!"

The tensions created by resistance to Church tyranny were not the product of agnosticism but of truth spread abroad by the Secret Society of Scripture-oriented men and women. They infiltrated the fabric of society by the thousands, and their recruiting practices were creative; they constantly marked gifted children for their teachings. Their meetings were clandestine and always consisted of Bible teaching, prayer, communion and tactics designed to avoid the authorities. The propagation of their doctrine demanded resistance to four principal points of the Church in Rome: 1) pilgrimages; 2) adoration of saints; 3) no reading of Scripture books in English; and 4) belief in the carnal presence of Christ's body in the Sacrament.

In the early years of the movement (1375-1435) the zeal of the Lollards manifested in varying degrees of boldness. Many of the young zealots refused to recant of their convictions when seized and tried by inquisitors. Their fate was often as not sealed by being publically burned at the stake. In western England in 1417 violence erupted under a militant zealot, John Oldcastle, who attempted to overthrow the tyranny of the Church. It aroused the monarch to squelch the rebellion by military force. Henceforth the Lollard movement went underground. Its numbers increased and their secrecy became sophisticated and gained converts throughout the social classes, especially in the merchant adventurers, whose wealth and power increased dramatically as England became a seafaring nation. Tactics for survival were drastically altered by the last half of the fifteenth century. Those in the Society now recanted when caught and avoided persecution by pleading ignorance of wrongdoing.

From what cloth were these men and women cut? What was the source of inspiration that led them to jeopardize their very lives and the lives of associates, friends and family?

Their spiritual father was John Wycliffe, the most exalted preacher in all of England during the fourteenth century. He was a professor of the Bible and president of Balliol College at Oxford. His fame as the most learned man of his time attracted students from the Continent and from all of England. His intolerance of Church abuses, begging friars, unlearned clergy, politically motivated bishops and inaccessibility of the Scriptures in the language of the common people, as well as the Church's demands on the monarch and its involvement in civil law and order, resulted in his championing the separation of church and state. Wycliffe was a mental giant well versed in law, theology, philosophy and logic. His criticism of Church practices regarding transubstantiation, taxation and toleration of ignorant clergy attracted the respect and admiration of the monarch. Anne of Bohemia (wife of King Richard) and John of Gaunt, Prince of Wales and monarch in absentia while King Richard was on a crusade to Jerusalem, were friends and admirers who protected Wycliffe from persecution by the Church hierarchy. His classrooms overflowed with disciples who were amazed at his logic and candor. Wycliffe was an imposing figure with his white hair and beard; he mocked and taunted the institution of the Church as a disgrace to God and to the people it "instructed" in the ways of God. Attempts were made to silence the fiery preacher; nevertheless, his friends in high places (and a timely earthquake that struck during his third trial for heresy) spared his life and enhanced his following.

Wycliffe's passion for translating the Latin Bible into the vernacular (Middle English) eventually resulted in his dismissal from Oxford. He set up shop at his parish church in Lutterworth in 1375, training his disciples to take God's Word to the people in the market place and on the way. His young preachers, called Lollards, would take handwritten portions of translated Scripture from village to village to read and instruct the people who gathered there. Only the well-educated could read and write, and without the printing press (yet to be invented) their task was slow. Their zeal, as often as not, was met by clerical resistance that resulted in severe persecution and death by

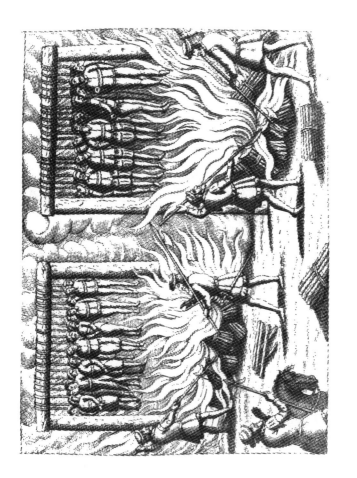

Divers Persons counted for Lollards hanged and burned in the first year of the reign of King Henry V, 1414.

fire. Wycliffe taught his "poor priests" to expect persecution and, if confronted, not to run from martyrdom. To send young men into harm's way was accepted by Wycliffe as a necessary sacrifice to awaken the masses and the monarchy.

The odds for awakening the ignorant masses in Wycliffe's lifetime were overwhelming, however. It took ten months to transcribe a whole Bible, and the undertaking was very expensive. Time was not on his side. On the last day of 1384, New Year's Eve, Wycliffe charged a follower with instructions to continue the work and joined the ranks of heavenly saints.

John Wycliffe was one man against the world. His role was to educate, recruit, write, defend and study. His strategically placed friends and students protected his flanks as he performed this role. He was a walking, talking Bible school. He was a doctor of doctors and was, truly, a *university* ("diversity in oneness") in the purest sense of the word. He illuminated the Scriptures for those who had ears to hear. The battle cry of his followers was, "If God be for us who can be against us?"(Rom. 8:31).

Wycliffe's zeal for nationalism and self-rule within the state lit the fires that John Huss would turn into an inferno on the Continent. Huss developed his theocracy and philosophy for nationalism by virtue of exchange students that were sponsored at Oxford by the Church in Prague between 1365 and 1375. The students wrote down every word that Wycliffe expounded in the classroom during their two-year courses, and Huss benefited from their notes. By the time Huss was tried for heresy by the Church, his doctrine had so influenced the people that the course he had set would never be reversed. How ironic was Huss' fate: his enemies burned him at the stake using his manuscripts from Wycliffe's lectures as kindling.

More than one hundred years later Martin Luther would benefit from Wycliffe's writings in England and Huss' accomplishments on the Continent, without which the German nationalistic pride that allowed Luther to resist and grow would certainly have been snuffed out by the might of the Roman Church. Tyndale would benefit from Wycliffe's love of God in a completely different way. Dismissing the need for an earthly advocate with God meant that Tyndale could have access to God even while in exile and without the assistance of the Church. Jesus Christ was the only Advocate to whom Tyndale pledged obedience.

Wycliffe's death brought a sigh of relief to the Church, which did not foresee the consequences of his life and his teachings. His epitaph is futuristic and is best stated by Simon, the son of Onias, in the book of Ecclesiasticus chapter 50: "Even as the Morning Star being in the midst of a cloud, and as the moon being full in her course, and as bright beams of the sun, so doth he shine and glister in the temple and church of God." Wycliffe earned and deserves history's claim, "The Morning Star of the Reformation."

Wycliffe's mantle was passed to John Purvey, who continued to transcribe into English biblical manuscripts and tracts designed to instruct the masses and re-establish the Church as it was in the first century. Purvey had lived with Wycliffe, absorbed his teaching, opinions and philosophy, and continued as his companion to his dying day. He filled the vacuum created by Wycliffe's death with tireless energy, courage and endurance, ensuring that his teacher had not died in vain.

One of Wycliffe's tracts, *The Wicket*, was circulated by the thousands in the years following his death. It promoted understanding of the sacrament of communion and brought the Lord's Supper back into the homes to be taught and observed as those Christians in the first century had done. John Purvey revised and accelerated the production of Wycliffe's English Bibles. The movement proliferated and many followers went underground as persecution by the Church intensified in its effort to stop what Wycliffe had given credibility in all classes of society.

The Lollards were zealous teachers of the gospel in their mother tongue. Their numbers multiplied as logarithmically as that of the followers of the apostle Paul had 1350 years previously. Portions of Wycliffe's sacred translation were circulated far and wide and became a textbook for the emerging English language. Chaucer's poetry is honored by misled historians as the basis for the English language. In truth, Chaucer was a confederate of Wycliffe and honored that great man with his "Tale of the Parson" in *The Canterbury Tales*. The gospel in the Middle English dialect served as a textbook for learning to thousands; by means of the Lollards, Wycliffe's writings and philosophy formed the foundation that educated peasants and scholars to nationalism and freedom. Wycliffe wrote in English and Latin, and his work was translated into the vernacular on the Continent as well.

Consider one example of Wycliffe's success in proliferating the Gospels. In June of 1394, Arundel, the Archbishop of York, preached the sermon at the funeral of Anne of Bohemia, Queen of Richard II. He spoke of her as being no stranger to the four Gospels in English and that, as a result of reading those books, she was "more learned than the prelates." Furthermore, Arundel had examined the books and declared them "to be good and true." This demonstrated that English translations had penetrated the palaces and were studied by royalty.

By 1408 the spread of Lollardism was causing great alarm in the Church. Fourteen years after he preached the funeral sermon, the Archbishop of York changed his mind and gathered the Church hierarchy at Oxford to discredit and ban Wycliffe's Bible.

We therefore decree and ordain, that from hence forth no unauthorized person shall translate any part of the Holy Scripture into English or any other language, under any form of book or treatise.

(Baxter's *Hexapla*, 1841)

The order and manner of taking away the body of John Wycliffe, and burning his bones forty-four years after his death.

This is the first and, indeed, the only authoritative prohibition of the English Scriptures, and it formed the basis of many subsequent persecutions. It was an instrument of terror suspended over the heads of all Englishmen who dared to read for themselves the Word of Life in their mother tongue.

Even after Wycliffe's death the hatred against his person continued to grow. Finally, in 1428, forty-four years after his death, Pope Martin V ordered the bones of Wycliffe to be dug up and burned. This inhuman act was done; Wycliffe's ashes were cast into the River Swift, a little stream running by the church in the town of Lutterworth.

The Lollards of the late fifteenth century and early sixteenth century were scattered throughout England and the Continent, and as the sixteenth century began and the New Learning was spread abroad, they continued to smuggle literature into the countryside of England and onto the Continent.

Essential to the proliferation of this new knowledge was the European invention of movable type in 1454 by Johannes Gutenberg in Mainz, Germany. Before his invention, it took months to draft a new book or Bible by hand. Therefore books were scarce. Martin Luther was over twenty years old before he held a Bible. Now the contest for the minds of men and women had the advantage of printing, with both the Church and the Reformers possessing the equipment to spread their doctrines.

Chapter 2

Colet and Erasmus

In 1453 Constantinople, the capitol of Eastern Orthodoxy, fell to the Turks. It was a tragedy for Eastern Orthodoxy but a blessing to the western world. Before the city fell, scholars and members of the upper class recognized their impending doom and fled to the West. They took with them their sacred codices and scrolls that described the ancient Greek culture of Plato, Socrates and Aristotle as well as unknown writings of the early church fathers. They also brought the Scriptures in their original language. The study of these manuscripts exposed the errors of the Latin Vulgate and kindled the fire for the New Learning.

By the sixteenth century a new generation had arrived who had imbibed the New Learning almost uncritically. They were more self-assured in their independence, more impatient in their opposition to obscurity and bigotry, and more ready to note how shallow resistance to all innovation often attracts the more learned opponents of innovation in letters and in doctrine.

This new generation in England was characterized by John Colet, Dean of St. Paul's Cathedral, who upon returning from Italy in 1496 took an irreversible path which let the Scriptures speak directly to the people in the pew for the first time. What was quite new in Colet's lectures was the theology of Paul, taught in English as translated from the original Greek, without any interpretation other than what Paul said.

Colet, the son of the Lord Mayor of London, had pursued his studies in Italy under Greek scholars able to teach the language in which the New Testament was written. The influence of Savonarola had placed a seal on Colet's life and lit a fire in his soul. Savonarola was a great preacher who called Italian culture back to Christianity, and that same preaching touched the life and soul of the visiting Englishman. Colet was an enthusiastic student of the Greek New Testament and made a history-altering decision to preach and teach when he returned to England.

Colet's subsequent lectures at Oxford were an epoch in the history of Bible exposition. He was intent on letting Paul speak for himself. Paul the apostle was a real person to Colet, and his lectures made Paul real to his audience. Colet recognized the need for the

The martyrdome of Jerome and his two companions.

Bible in the language of the people. It is certain that without his political connections in government he would have suffered martyrdom for his innovations. There also can be little doubt of Colet's influence on the early education of William Tyndale.

Since Origen, an early church father of the third century, it had been automatic in the Church, much influenced by Augustine, to treat every sentence and often every word of the Latin Scripture as allegorical. On top of the first meaning, the literal, were piled the allegorical (animals, for example, suggesting virtues); the tropological or moral, involving tropes (figures) of morality and the anagogical, (from the Greek word meaning "to rise"), that is "elevatory" especially to future glory. The most famous example of this old school biblical exegesis is the word "Jerusalem," which literally means "the city of the Jews"; allegorically, "the church of Christ"; tropologically, "the human soul" and anagogically, "the heavenly city." The results of this manner of exegesis rendered the theology of Paul as very mystical for the common man and often perverted the very meaning of the apostle's words. Colet brushed aside the treatment of the Bible as a verbally inspired arsenal of texts; he would have nothing to do with the Church's neglect of the literal sense in favor of the allegorical, tropological and anagogical interpretations.

Colet's approach would never have left the hallowed halls of Oxford or the cathedral walls of St.

Paul's were it not for the divine providence that brought Erasmus of Rotterdam under his influence and, in so doing, thrust that learned man onto the stage of world history.

Erasmus was an intellectual diplomat who managed to walk the fine line between advocating reform and being accused of heretical teaching among the Reformers. However, he became a champion of the Reformers' zeal to translate Scripture into a language that the commoners, both men and women, could understand. He was the ultimate opportunist who pushed academic freedom to its limits whenever the occasion arose. Erasmus was untouchable insofar as the critics of the New Learning were concerned. The friendship of Sir Thomas More and others in powerful positions permitted him excesses at Oxford and later at Cambridge that left an indelible mark on the progressive teaching of Greek at both universities. Even so, he had detractors and critics, especially in England. It is acknowledged that Erasmus' passion to compile and print a Greek New Testament was all his critics needed to have him expelled from Cambridge in 1514. Not even his association with More and other Church leaders, or his powerful chair at the university could insulate him from the threat of trial or imprisonment for his passion and zeal to print a Greek-Latin Bible. So he went to Basel, a city-state in modern Switzerland tolerant of the New Learning, and never returned to England.

In the autumn of 1515, Froben, a Swiss scholar and printer, contracted with Erasmus to issue the New

Testament in Greek. Froben knew that a scholarly work of the Greek Testament was then at the press in Spain under the tutelage of the powerful Cardinal Ximenes, the Archbishop of Toledo. In 1514 Ximenes had completed the New Testament from a more complete collection of Greek manuscripts than that of Erasmus, which made his collation possible; nevertheless, Ximenes was intent on a polyglot Bible comprising a Septuagint (the Old and New Testaments in Greek), a Hebrew Old Testament and a Latin translation of the whole—a colossal work as a final product—which delayed the printing until 1518. His hesitation to print the New Testament alone was the opening that Froben anticipated.

In 1516, two years before Ximenes completed his work, Froben and Erasmus issued *The Greek New Testament*, the first lawful Greek-Latin Bible in a millennium. The text was rough, possessing errors in printing that were the result of haste and incomplete Greek manuscripts. The manuscripts were supplied by Froben (except for two that were loaned to Erasmus by Colet from the library at St. Paul's) and in reality were so incomplete that they did not make up the equivalent of one entire Testament; furthermore, the manuscripts were relatively recent, the oldest being tenth century. Because of this incompleteness, Erasmus finished his Greek translation from the Vulgate.

Erasmus printed the Greek alongside his own translation in Latin and, in the process, struck a death blow to the Vulgate. He introduced prefatory notes that fueled the fires for reform and, as a result of the lights that John Colet had lit in him seventeen years earlier, established Paul as the New Testament authority concerning the church and its relationship to the non-ecclesiastical participant, the layman.

Erasmus was considered the outstanding scholar of his time. The following exhortation in the Preface of his New Testament demonstrates his courage at the critical hour:

> I utterly dissent from those who are unwilling that the sacred Scriptures should be read by the unlearned translated into their own vulgar tongue.

> I wish that even the weakest woman should read the Gospels, should read the Epistles of St. Paul. I long that the husbandman should sing some portion of them to himself as he follows the plough.

Erasmus and Froben were aware of the weaknesses in their work; nevertheless, demand was overwhelming. The horse was out of the proverbial barn and the door closed too late. Response to the Greek-Latin Testament proliferated and Froben's presses ran night and day. The profits were large enough to underwrite revisions as well as to fund projects that were essential to the Reformers' need for supportive literature in defense of their new movement.

Had he possessed a daring spirit, Erasmus might have used his position to lead. But the world of action was not his world. He could prepare the ground but not harvest the crop. His passive resistance belies his name in the annals of the Reformation; others would reap where he had sown. Although Erasmus was careful and felt that discretion was the better part of valor, his words were read and never forgotten by Tyndale who, as we shall see, sacrificed his life in making them come true.

The "undesigned coincidences" that took place during the first sixteen years of the sixteenth century make a truly remarkable story with an equally fascinating end among those who were emerging with a burden to throw off the bondage of tyranny. The collaboration of Froben with Erasmus on this project ensured proliferation of the Greek text, for Erasmus' participation stalled the critics' condemnation. Erasmus was the most brilliant man of letters of the century, already known and admired by the Church hierarchy from Oxford to Rome. It was typical of Erasmus that, even where he promoted a revolutionary change, he was careful to maintain the outward forms of decorum. Thus his most radical acts never led to a confrontation or collision with the ecclesiastical hierarchy. This consummate diplomat dedicated the first free translation of the Greek-Latin New Testament to Pope Leo X. In response, Leo spoke those essential words of respect, dispelling Erasmus' fears, "We are greatly pleased."

In spite of Erasmus' scholarly reputation on the Continent and inside the Vatican, England would not permit the circulation of his New Testament. England had been the birthplace for the idea of his translation; nevertheless, the forces of conservatism would not tolerate its fulfillment on her soil. Neither the Greek nor the English text would be printed first in England.

Chapter 3

Early Life of Tyndale

"One million dollars is the bid: Going once, going twice, sold! to the group from Japan."

Thus the sale of a first edition (1623) of Shakespeare's plays brought applause from the gallery of millionaires from around the world. The year was 1990. The place, Quaritch's Auction House in London.

Several years ago seven times that amount was offered to Baptist College in Bristol, England, for a small New Testament printed in 1525 by William Tyndale, the man who translated the 1522 edition of Erasmus' Greek New Testament into English for the first time. In the process, William Tyndale gave to his native England its language and its code of ethics for her posterity.

This Bible in English is the product of one man working alone. The persistence of William Tyndale's work is, in fact, the outstanding miracle in the history of English letters. His words are daily on our lips, his phrases are part of our speech, his cadences are treasured in every part of the world where the English language has gone. What other Englishman has touched so many lives?

The father of the English language, the sole translator of the Bible into modern English must certainly be revered by every Christian, every English-speaking man or woman, boy and girl, wherever the Bible is studied and wherever English is taught as either history or literature. In fact, however, his biography has never been published in America; his life and work are scarcely known to the intellectual community, much less to the common masses. Surely he lived and died in honor and wealth and was respected by all? Tyndale's own words describe his true plight as he stood in a field outside the gates of Antwerp in 1531 under the cover of darkness:

> If for my pains therein taken, if for my poverty, if for my exile out of my natural country, and bitter absence from my friends, if for my hunger, my thirst, my cold, the great danger wherewith I am everywhere compassed, and finally, if for my innumerable other hard and sharp fightings which I endure....

To the establishment, William Tyndale was an outlaw. He had a price on his head and was hunted relentlessly for eleven years by his king and by the Church. His only crime was Christian obedience to God, and thus resistance to tyranny.

Little is known of William Tyndale's childhood, but it is believed he was born in 1494 in Gloucestershire, near Bristol. From 1494 to 1505 he grew up in one of the most naturally beautiful areas of England. In Gloucestershire, a county in the west of England, agriculture was the main occupation; however, its proximity to Bristol, the second largest port in England (after London), made it possible to monitor the exciting events occurring in the world with each arriving ship.

He enrolled at Oxford in 1505 and literally grew up at the university, receiving his M.A. (Master's degree) in 1515 at the age of twenty-three. It was not unusual for a young man demonstrating a keen mind to begin his studies at an early age. He proved to be a gifted linguist, as testified by an associate of later years in Germany. This associate described Tyndale as "so skilled in seven tongues, Hebrew, Greek, Latin, Italian, Spanish, English, French [German is taken for granted] that whichever he speaks you might think it is his native tongue." This gift must have been useful in his successful evasion of the authorities during his exile from England.

John Foxe records in his famous *Book of Martyrs* that Tyndale's days at Oxford were normal and, for the most part, uneventful:

Brought up from a child in the University of Oxford, where he, by long continuance, grew up, and increased as well in the knowledge of tongues and other liberal arts, as especially in the knowledge of Scriptures, whereunto his mind was singularly addicted: insomuch that he, lying then in Magdalen Hall, read privily to certain students and fellows of Magdalen College some parcel of divinity; instructing them in the knowledge of the truth of the Scriptures. His manners also and conversation being correspondent to the same, were such that all that knew him reputed and esteemed him to be a man of most virtuous disposition and of life unspotted. Thus he, in the University of Oxford, increasing more and more in learning and proceeding in degrees of the schools, spying his time, removed from thence to the University of Cambridge

A seven-year course was required to earn an M.A. The subjects of the study were the Seven Liberal Arts: Grammar, Rhetoric and Logic (the Trivium) and Music, Arithmetic, Geometry and Astronomy (the Quadrennium). In addition, the course included the more serious studies of the Three Philosophies: Natural, Moral and Metaphysical. This curriculum was designed to teach the mind to think.

During these years the influence of Colet's lectures on the apostle Paul's writings and the New Learning in general must have had an exciting impact on William Tyndale and his fellow students. As early as 1491 Bishop Russell had despaired of the influence of Lollardy at Oxford; therefore, the possibility of William Tyndale being influenced by the Secret Society is distinct. Not only did he learn Greek, but he also shared fully in a revulsion for the Schoolmen, the conservative clergy. So, eager to study the Bible without their rules and glosses, he abandoned the pursuit of a degree in divinity.

A witch hunt, conducted by Cardinal Wolsey at Oxford for forbidden books, was a cause of great alarm in 1516 and 1517, and probably influenced William Tyndale to move on to more tolerant territory. His next stop was Cambridge University and the White Horse Inn Society. This Society was composed of about twenty-five young men, most of whom would burn at the stake in succeeding decades and in the process awaken the monarch and the masses to their cause.

In 1517 at Little Park in Coventry five men and two women were tried for heresy. The charge was teaching their children the Lord's Prayer and the Ten Commandments in English. They were found guilty and burned at the stake in the public square. Although these poor souls were not members of the ecclesiastical establishment, their martyrdom spoke clearly of the insanity that had possessed the Church. The Reformers had to exercise great care for their own lives.

Outside the walls of Cambridge, faculty and students met at an ale house plotting the overthrow of the Roman Church and its influence in England. The White Horse Inn was nicknamed "Little Germany," thus, by its very name, causing little doubt of the topic of conversation shared by its patrons.

By 1521 Cambridge was becoming as uncomfortable as Oxford. It was difficult to predict who one's friends were. Under such a cloud of constant tension and fear, Tyndale sought time to consider the expediting of his mission to translate the Bible into English. Almost thirty years old and well spoken of by his peers for his knowledge and ability to expound Scriptures, Tyndale returned to the neighborhood of his birth to the service of Sir John Walsh at the manor house of Little Sodbury in the Cotswolds north of Bristol. His assignment to the Walsh family was to tutor their two children and be chaplain to Sir John and his wife.[1]

Sir John Walsh was a champion of Henry VIII and married Anne Poyntz, whose family was well known and respected in Gloucestershire. The influence of Lollardy was subtle in the manor. Sir John opened the

---

1. The manor house survives today and the very room where Tyndale slept and worked is still kept clean and neat. In the second story room a window allows a magnificent panorama of the Severn Valley where farmers tend their fields, reminiscent of the plow-boys of the sixteenth century that Tyndale looked upon from his desk as he studied and first attempted English translations from the Latin and Greek.

Seven godly martyrs burned in Coventry.

estate to the bishops and clergy of the diocese for dinners and table-talk and regularly invited beneficed men, abbots, deans and archdeacons. Sir John showed off his new tutor and chaplain, encouraging debate and argument, for he desired to rightly influence the power brokers of his area to the truth of Scriptures. The talks revealed the depths of superstition and ignorance, and confirmed to Tyndale his belief that the Bible in the hands of the people was the only cure for the degradation of the Church.

It is certain that the exchanges in the dining room grew heated with time. Always Tyndale expounded the meaning of Scripture as the final authority and standard during arguments that would continue for hours. His frustration precipitated dangerous statements that threatened the participants and caused distress to Lady Walsh, who admired and respected her guests for their position and power in the community. Finally, she confronted Tyndale for his boldness in demanding authority of Scripture with the notion that his position, which was defended by her husband, was making her and the guests very uncomfortable. After all, how could a poor tutor like Tyndale refute the opinions of such powerful and wealthy men that God had honored by placing them over the common people? Her sincere naivete was a cause of deep concern to Tyndale, and he understood the merits of her anguish. In essence, he had to face the facts: The mere words of Scripture quoted by him carried no weight, whereas everyone would heed the teaching of the greatest scholar in Christendom, Erasmus.

Tyndale's response to Lady Walsh was carefully sought and prayerfully undertaken. From the library at the manor Tyndale exploited the writings of Erasmus to address her distress. The earliest and most daring work of Erasmus was *The Manual of a Christian Knight* written in Latin twenty years previously. Erasmus had in youthful honesty attacked the abuses of the Church, and in so doing kindled great debate among the literate. Tyndale undertook the English translation of this work and, in the process, not only won over his benefactor to the cause but also honed his skill and built his confidence for the larger task God had set before him. His English translation painted a picture of the truth to Lady Walsh as page after page confirmed his own position. Erasmus had written, "Christ has not died in order that wealth, abundance, arms, and the rest of the pomp of an earthly kingdom which was formerly possessed by the heathen should now be in the possession of a few priests not unlike heathens." His attack on the clergy for wasting time on useless debate instead of teaching the people, in simple language, the religion of Christ, demanded the authority of the New Testament alone for the standard of Christian living, not Church laws and observances.

No longer was William Tyndale's opinion questioned by Sir John and Lady Walsh and no longer was the grand clergy received. It is not surprising that Tyndale created a bitterness among future enemies in high places, who could undermine his mission if he were not careful.

Tyndale's confidence grew and, under the protection of Sir John, he launched his preaching in the villages and on the college grounds in Bristol. Tyndale's teaching caused a feeling of insecurity among the clergy and in 1523 a subpoena from the acting bishop of the diocese demanded a hearing. Tyndale said of the confrontation: "He reviled me like I was a dog." However, his position in the service of Sir John and his own defense neutralized the charges, so he avoided being branded a heretic or taking the oath of abjuration. It was a close call.

Discretion was the order of the day. William Tyndale exercised restraint when dealing with his clerical counterparts who were woefully ignorant of the Bible. He grew increasingly convinced of the necessity for Scriptures in English that, by the power of God, could correct the errors of the Church. Equally, the need for the Scriptures in a printed form that the common man and woman could understand weighed heavily on his mind.

Although Tyndale restricted his teaching to more friendly confines, he was not devoid of confrontation. After the passage of time, given to much thought as to the consequences of his intended path, a circumstance prompted an argument which demanded a rebuttal. A certain clergyman taunted Tyndale with the statement, "We were better to be without God's laws than the Pope's." Imprudence drove Tyndale to correct the "learned" man by proclaiming, "I defy the

Pope and all his laws. If God spare my life ere many years, I will cause the boy that drives the plow to know more of the Scriptures than you."

His mind was made up. He had to acquire permission to translate the Scriptures into English. The burden of his soul was revealed, and his friends and associates were in danger of being implicated. With the assistance of Sir John Walsh, through the means of letters and recommendations, he would seek the Bishop of London's favor to undertake the translation of the Bible into English. With a spirit of optimism, Tyndale began his great adventure.

Tyndale arrived in London in July or August of 1523. He carried the proper papers of introduction as well as a recent English translation of an oration of Isocrates to demonstrate to Bishop Tunstal his skill in translating the Greek. After all, Tunstal was commended by Erasmus as a proficient and wise scholar; furthermore, Sir John Walsh had friends in the bishop's household who could expedite an interview.

The task at hand was complicated by bureaucratic red tape, but Tyndale was energized and patient. He used the time to observe and to make new acquaintances, particularly among the Secret Society. A great debate was being conducted in Parliament, which was in session for the first time in seven years. Henry VIII wanted money, and his exorbitant demands were being resisted by the House of Commons even though Cardinal Wolsey had personally gone to them to appeal for the king. Tyndale was appalled at the Cardinal's conduct in matters of the state and later spoke of "Wolfsey" as the "falsest and vainest Cardinal that ever was."

Bishop Tunstal's house was full of zealous graduates from Oxford and Cambridge who were eager to please and "play the game." Tyndale saw his mistake in believing the ecclesiastical powers of London to be any more spiritual than those of Rome. At this point in his life he had to be confused about the accomplishment of his burden. It was dawning on him that there was no place in all of England to undertake the translation and printing of the Bible in English.

Tyndale's new friends in London's Secret Society included Humphrey Monmouth, a merchant adventurer in whose house he resided and preached. The "brotherhood" was active in the city, and ample opportunity was afforded to strategize his burden. There were churches where Tyndale spoke and ministered, and he had enough study time to solidify his purpose. Monmouth was probably a friend of Tyndale's family in the west and provided the hospitality that Tyndale needed in order to acquaint himself with people who would be essential to the success of his future accomplishments on the Continent.

William Tyndale bided his time, waiting for the opportunity to commence his translation. He knew what God wanted him to do. The writings of Martin Luther were discussed in secret, and the translation of the German New Testament was undoubtedly accessible to him. The consensus that England was not the place to translate and print an English Bible was apparent. The test of Tyndale's purpose rested in his willingness to exile himself to the Continent, thereby forsaking friends and family.

As difficult as things were in England, the Continent was a war zone of upheaval of much more drastic and widespread persecution. During the Spanish Inquisition, 31,912 people were burned and 291,450 were imprisoned in Spain alone. Italy, France and Portugal were little better. Only in Germany and the Low Countries were there pockets of freedom to question the pope's sole authority on earth. Armed with this knowledge, Tyndale chose Hamburg as his venue to undertake the translation of the English Bible. In May of 1524 he set sail, never to look on his beloved homeland again.

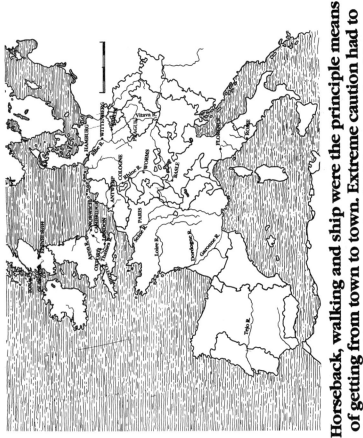

Horseback, walking and ship were the principle means of getting from town to town. Extreme caution had to be used when going overland. Thieves and robbers were a real threat to anyone perceived as well-to-do.

Chapter 4

The First English Bible

After he landed in Hamburg in May 1524, we can with reasonable certainty follow William Tyndale's movements for the remainder of his life. Humphrey Monmouth had agreed to financially support his efforts, and a system of secret communication was worked out between the men so that Tyndale could receive the needed finances to underwrite the work as it progressed. The Lollards were very active, but secrecy was essential and movement from town to town was carefully concealed from the Inquisitors.

The headquarters for the Reformation resided in Wittenberg with Martin Luther. It had been seven years since Luther nailed the 95 Theses to the door of the Castle Church in Wittenberg. With the printing press working day and night, the 95 Theses had been distributed all over Germany and the Continent. In 1520 the pope issued a papal bull of excommunication to Luther, who, with great ceremony, burned it in a public demonstration of his defiance on December 10, 1520. Luther had determined that the sole authority was the Scriptures, not the pope.

On January 6, 1521, the Diet of Worms convened. Luther was summoned with a guarantee of safe conduct. On April 16 he entered the city to meet his accusers with their demands for his retraction of his views. Luther responded to their demands on April 17: "Unless I am convinced by proofs from Scriptures or by plain and clear reasons and arguments, I can and will not retract, for it is neither safe nor wise to do anything against conscience." And then, looking around the assembly, he said—and the words are among the most sublime in history—"Here I stand. I cannot do otherwise. God help me! Amen!"

Luther's life and work are legendary, and ill taught in America even to this day. For reasons that are clearly logical, Luther was a man whom Tyndale had to meet. Sometime in the fall of 1524 and winter of 1525 the two did meet, and as a consequence the world was never again the same. Martin Luther majored on the message of Paul, primarily through Paul's epistles to the Romans and Galatians. The gospel message was essential for the salvation of man, according to Luther's understanding and interpretation, and all else was *adiaphora* (nonessential). Tyndale embraced

Luther's theology as would his native England in future generations as a result of his translating into English Luther's pioneering efforts.

With all its subtleties, the influence of Lollardy in Luther's life had elevated him to the stature of giant-killer. The course was set on the Continent for William Tyndale because Luther had challenged the authority of the Church and lived to tell the tale. What confronted Tyndale at Wittenberg excites the imagination. The German New Testament had been circulated throughout the nation of Charles V, much to the chagrin of Pope Clement VII. The princes who held power in their respective states could not be coerced to military confrontation against Prince Philip, who protected Luther. Even Charles, a puppet of the pope, recognized that a civil war would weaken the nation against the threat from the Turks.

Although the situation was unstable and tenuous to say the least, Prince Philip championed Luther. As long as Luther was careful, his day-to-day existence was free from reprisal. His presses ran day and night, circulating literature far and wide via the merchant adventurers like Monmouth, who risked their lives with every sailing to transport their forbidden contraband. Luther was surrounded by such brillance as Melanchthon and Spalatin. By 1529 the protest reached a level that demanded everyone should be protected in the exercise of his religion, whatever form of faith or worship he might choose to adopt. Hence, the name *Protestant* was coined, which simply meant those who were separated from the Church of Rome.

By the time William Tyndale met with Luther in 1524 or 1525, "Justification by Faith," the prologue to Romans, had been refined and embraced as the cornerstone for the foundation of the new movement. Within Luther's sphere of influence, theocratic obstacles were cleared so that men and women could, by faith, accept salvation on the merits of Christ's work, obedience and sacrifice alone. Indulgences were not accepted as a means to remit the penalty of sin. Luther knew that sin was a matter between the heavenly Father and His child, and it was a travesty of the relationship to teach that the paying of money could restore a person to God's favor.

Tyndale left Wittenberg in the autumn of 1525. It is likely that the largest part of the New Testament was already translated, at least in rough draft form. It is equally realistic to suppose that Luther and Tyndale had plotted the strategy necessary to have an effect on England and its belligerent monarch. Without question, what Luther had started would fail in succeeding generations if England remained loyal to Rome. It was extremely important for the English New Testament to get into print. It was the priority.

Cologne was the jumping-off port for Tyndale and his associate, William Roye. The fact that Cologne was a Roman Catholic city evidences the psychology of their strategy. The enemy would not expect the Bible in English to originate from that direction, whereas Wittenberg was the hotbed for forbidden literature. In addition, Peter Quentel, the most famous printer in Germany, was sympathetic to the Reformers and willing and able to undertake the job in Cologne.

Secrecy was of the essence, and in the early stages of the process contact between Quentel and Tyndale was made largely by go-betweens to avoid arousing suspicion. The work quickly progressed to the extent that three thousand copies of the New Testament were in the press—a quarto edition with prologue, marginal notes and references. The Gospel of Matthew was complete, and Tyndale had more than enough money to complete the printing and binding.

At this juncture disaster struck. Rumors had circulated that the Bible was being printed in English and that soon all of England would come under Lutheran influence in spite of king and cardinal. A certain Roman bounty hunter caught wind of these rumors and invited some printers to dine with him. After a few hours of food and spirits, Cochlaeus' suspicions were confirmed. He learned that the New Testament was being printed at Peter Quentel's shop, and that the work was being undertaken by two Englishmen skilled in languages. Cochlaeus notified the authorities of the printing of forbidden books bound for England, and the town senate issued an order for Quentel to cease and desist.

Tyndale and Roye were tipped off about the senate order. Only minutes ahead of Cochlaeus, who was seeking to confiscate the printed material, they snatched the printed sheets and escaped up the Rhine River to Worms. The disappointment had to be excruciating, but Tyndale regrouped in Worms at the print shop of Peter Schoeffer, the son of the partner of Johannes Gutenberg. There the job was again undertaken, this time without the threat of confiscation, and in the latter days of 1525 the complete New Testament was printed in some thousands of copies. The forbidden books were smuggled into England by merchant adventurers in the late winter and spring of 1525-26 in bags of flour and bales of cloth received at the port of London. The printing was a revision of the New Testament attempted at Cologne, but was one-half the size (octavo).

Of the thousands printed at Worms only two copies remain: one copy lacking only the title page at Baptist College in Bristol and a fragment in the library of St. Paul's Cathedral in London. The completed Gospel of Matthew from the Cologne printing was not seen again for three hundred years and was assumed lost until 1836, when an English bookseller found it bound in another book. Today that fragment of the first printing of the English New Testament is one of the priceless possessions of the British Museum.

Cochlaeus had sent a warning to Henry VIII and Cardinal Wolsey that illegal Bibles printed in English were on their way. An alert was given, but the merchants were too clever for the authorities. Smuggled copies were received by members of the Secret Society and distributed throughout the country. In October of 1526 Bishop Tunstal preached a sermon at St. Paul's Cross denouncing the New Testament in English, and copies were publicly burned. The authorities claimed that they burned the Bibles because they were filled with errors; in fact, they were burned because they could find no errors.

No better means of creating interest in the New Testament could have been devised. The English became a Bible-minded people, and the mystery of the forbidden New Testament in English created a demand that no amount of advertising could have accomplished. The frustration of the monarch and the church leaders resulted in massive missions to track down the books and prosecute those found possessing them. The success of their fervent search is manifested by the scarcity of Tyndale's original printing.

The Story of Augustine Pakington

It was quite clear that the authorities could not prevent the entrance of the Book into England. And then a brilliant thought occurred to the Bishop of London. He sought out Augustine Pakington, a merchant trading to Antwerp, and asked his opinion about buying up all the copies across the water.

"My Lord," replied Pakington, who was a secret friend of Tyndale's, "if it be your pleasure I could do in this matter probably more than any merchant in England; so if it be your Lordship's pleasure to pay for them—for I must disburse money for them—I will insure you to have every book that remains unsold."

"Gentle Master Pakington," said the bishop, deeming that he had God by the toe, when in truth he had, as after he thought, the devil by the fist, "do your diligence and get them for me, and I will gladly give you whatever they may cost, for the books are naughty, and I intend surely to destroy them all, and to burn them at Paul's Cross."

A few weeks later Pakington sought the translator, whose funds he knew were at a low ebb.

"Master Tyndale," he said, "I have found you a good purchase for your books."

"Who is he?" asked Tyndale.

"My lord of London."

"But if the bishop wants the books it must be only to burn them."

"Well," was the reply, "what of that? The bishop will burn them anyhow, and it is best that you should have the money for enabling you to imprint others instead."

And so the bargain was made. The bishop had the books, Pakington had the thanks and Tyndale had the money.

"I am the gladder," quoth Tyndale, "for these two benefits shall come thereof. I shall get money to bring myself out of debt, and the whole world will cry out against the burning of God's Word, and the overplus of the money that shall remain with me shall make me more studious to correct the said New Testament, and so newly to imprint the same once again, and I trust the second will be much better than ever was the first."

The story goes on: After this Tyndale corrected the same Testaments again, and caused them to be newly imprinted, so that they came thick and threefold into England. The bishop sent for Pakington again and asked how the Testaments were still so abundant. "My lord," replied the merchant, "it were best for your lordship to buy up the stamps too by which they were imprinted."

It is with evident enjoyment that the old chronicler presents to us another scene as a sequel to the story. A prisoner, a suspected heretic named Constantine, was being tried a few months later before Sir Thomas More.

"Now Constantine," said the judge, "I would have thee to be plain with me in one thing that I shall ask and I promise thee I will show thee favor in all other things whereof thou art accused. There are beyond the sea Tyndale, Joye, and a great many of you; I know they cannot live without help. There must be some that help and succor them with money, and thou, being one of them, hadst thy part thereof, and therefore knowest from when it came. I pray thee, tell me who be they that help them thus."

"My lord," quoth Constantine, "I will tell thee truly—it is the Bishop of London that hath holpen us, for he hath bestowed among us a great deal of money upon New Testaments to burn them, and that hath been our chief succor and comfort."

"Now by my troth," quoth Sir Thomas More, "I think even the same, for I told the bishop thus much before he went about it."

What had William Tyndale accomplished by publishing the New Testament in English?

Like John Colet twenty-five years before, who had let Paul speak in his sermons at Oxford and then at St. Paul's, William Tyndale had let Paul, Matthew, Mark, Luke and John speak as the authorities for the Christian and for the Church. Tyndale's translation was his own, for he had no help except the Holy Spirit in determining the thought and context of the passages.

The prologues to the books of the New Testament and the marginal references were in large measure borrowed from Luther's German New Testament. William Tyndale translated from Erasmus' Greek-Latin edition of 1522, from Luther's German New Testament and from the Latin Vulgate. He carefully compared texts with one another, always rendering the English closest to the Greek. He said of the overall effort, "I had no man to counterfeit [imitate] neither was helped with English of any that had interpreted the same or such like thing in the Scriptures afore time."

Tyndale was aware of the shortcomings of his translation. Time was of the essence. The New Testament had to be printed and distributed if England were to be gained for the Reformation. In his address to the "Most Dear Reader" he says, "Count it as a thing not having his full shape, but as it were born afore his time, even as a thing begun rather than finished. In time to come, if God has appointed us there unto, we will give it its full shape."

Tyndale was a gifted scholar and was never content with the final printed product. In 1534 he completely revised his text to a form that would comprise ninety percent of the King James Version of 1611, a work undertaken seventy years later by more than fifty scholars over a five-year period with unlimited funds and resources and the support of the king. Tyndale's original translation was completed in one year while in hiding with a price on his head and with the help of a single aide.

Tyndale's vision was to communicate a picture of salvation to the reader. In the process, the language had to be restructured and ordered so that its thought was most easily assimilated. William Tyndale styled the flow, at times poetically, that permitted the reader to readily commit the text to memory.

Dr. T.R. Glover calls that greatest achievement "speech that reaches the heart of man and lives there forever."

Dr. Westcott says, "He lifted up the common language to the grand simplicity of his own idiom."

His language was always plain, simple and direct. We owe a debt to the man who rendered the text in a style that helps forward the thought, evoking the proper emotional response whether in the Christmas story (Luke 2), the Great Commission (Matt. 28:19-20), or "For God so loved the world" (John 3:16). It is difficult to estimate what our spiritual loss would have been if the translation of the New Testament that set the standard for the future translations, as well as English speech in general, had been slipshod or pedantic.

William Tyndale experienced the struggles of life as the apostles and New Testament writers of the first century did. Their anguish and denial were his own. His loneliness, hunger and discomfort from the elements were communicated from first-hand experience. His faith was born of their faith, and he sought to communicate that to those at home in England who were suffering the persecutions of an unstable monarch and of a demonic clergy whose weapons of torture and death were more sophisticated than those of the first century Caesar. He would have said it was the Spirit of God who gave him the words and phrases that made the experiences of the first century live again in his language of translation.

Chapter 5

Chains of Freedom

In the city of Norwich, in eastern England, a memorial on the side of a pub pays homage to three hundred Lollards who were burned at the stake between 1390 and 1550. The site is called the Lollard's Pit, and it is the very place where the first English convert to the Reformation was burned at the stake in 1531. We remember him in this book because it is very likely that this man led William Tyndale to his calling. He is hardly a household word in either England or America, but his importance should not be underestimated. His name was Thomas Bilney, a pioneer of the English Reformation.

In 1517, a young divinity student at Cambridge, confused and physically spent from wrestling with his "lost condition," in a state of panic and desperation, left his dormitory room inside Trinity Hall one evening and made his way to a bookshop where "forbidden books" were sold. He purchased a copy of Erasmus' Greek-Latin New Testament. Hiding that night under a cover with his illegal purchase and a flickering candle, he felt the strong light of God pour into his soul, and the Reformation in England was officially born.

His testimony has come down to us in his confession to Bishop Tunstal in 1527:

> So that there was but small force of strength left in my body (who by nature was weak), small store of money, and very little wit or understanding; for they appointed me fasting, watching, buying of pardons and money. But at last I heard speak of Jesus even then when the New Testament was first set forth by Erasmus: which when I understood to be eloquently done by him, being allured rather by the Latin through the Word of God at that time I knew not what it meant, I bought it even by the Providence of God (as I do now well understand and perceive): and at the first reading (as I well remember) I chanced upon the sentence of St. Paul (O most sweet and comfortable sentence to my soul) in 1 Tim. 1:15, "It is a true saying and worthy of all men to be embraced that Jesus Christ came into the world to save sinners, of whom I am the chief and principal." This one sentence, through God's instruction and inward working,

which I did not then perceive, did so exhilarate my heart, being before wounded with the guilt of my sins, and being almost in despair, that even immediately I seemed unto myself inwardly to feel a marvelous comfort and quietness, insomuch that my bruised bones leaped for joy.

Unable to contain his newfound freedom from years of bondage, Thomas Bilney shared his experience with all who would give him their ears. His list of converts bears witness to his own genuine conversion. Over the next two years Bilney worked among his fellow scholars and friends in the university. Not only did Tyndale cross his path and join the Society at the White Horse Inn, but Hugh Latimer, the most promising young orator at the university, was also among the converts. In 1519 Bilney was ordained a priest and received his license to preach. At the same time Latimer gave an oration, choosing for his Bachelor of Divinity Act to attack the recently published work, *The Rhetoric* by Philip Melanchthon. After the oration, for which Latimer received accolades and a standing ovation from his peers, Bilney approached the young, gifted orator and asked "Father" Latimer to hear his confession. Latimer later wrote an account of this meeting:

Bilney sought me out, and he came to me afterwards in my study and desired me for God's sake to hear his confession: and to say the truth, by his confession I learned more than afore in many years. So from this time forward I began to smell the Word of God and forsook the school doctors and all such fooleries.

Bilney taught, preached and witnessed for ten years from Norwich to London to Cambridge. He became a powerful force to distribute Tyndale's new English Bible and other forbidden literature throughout England. On that account, the confession given to Tunstal in 1527 was on charges of heresy, preaching Lutheranism and distributing forbidden books. Bilney was incarcerated at the Tower of London and encouraged by his friends to recant. Twenty witnesses were assembled to support the prosecuting inquisitors, and as was the law, Bilney could not bring any witnesses on his own behalf. Bishop Tunstal administered the necessary torture, and in time Bilney did recant. His penance was to ignite the fire that would burn the New Testaments recently bought by Tunstal with Augustine Pakington's help. Bilney remained in the Tower for several months as further penance and became inconsolable because he had betrayed Tyndale and the cause. When he returned to Cambridge at the end of 1528, his spirit was broken and he was much distressed. Latimer recorded his concern for Bilney:

Little Bilney, that blessed martyr of God, what time he had borne his kindling and was come again to Cambridge had such conflicts within himself beholding this image of death, that his friends were afraid to let him alone. They were eager to be with him day and night and comforted him as they could; but no comforts would serve. As for the comfortable places of Scripture, to bring unto him it was as though a man would run him through the heart with a sword.

Bilney took action in his despair; one evening he left Cambridge, telling his friends he was "going up to Jerusalem." In the weeks to come he preached and distributed Bibles and books. He was arrested, "tried" and burned at the stake in the Lollard's Pit at Norwich while in his arms he embraced William Tyndale's *Obedience Of A Christian Man*. On a sunny day in August they made an end of the pioneer of the Reformation, but they as soon could end his cause as the sunshine.

Bilney encouraged his friends the night before his burning with these words: "Though the fire should be of great heat to my body, yet the comfort of God's spirit should cool it to my everlasting refreshing." At this point Bilney put his hand toward the flame of the candle burning before them and, feeling the heat said, "O, I feel by experience, and have known it long by philosophy, that fire by God's ordinance is naturally hot, but yet I am persuaded by God's Holy Word, and by the experience of some spoken of in the same, and in the fire they felt no consumption: and I constantly believe, howsoever that the stubble of this my body shall be wasted by it, yet my soul and spirit shall be

**Mr. Thomas Bilney
proving the fire with his finger.**

The burning of the godly and constant martyr, Mr. Thomas Bilney.

purged thereby; a pain for the time, whereon notwithstanding followeth joy unspeakable." And Bilney quoted, "Fear not, for I have redeemed thee, and called thee by thy name, thou art mine own. When thou goest through the water I will be with thee, and the strong floods shall not overflow thee. When thou walkest in the fire, it shall not burn thee, and the flame shall not kindle thee, for I am the Lord thy God, the Holy One of Israel" (Is. 43:1-3).

It was a time for patience. All wars are fought with courage, and in the heat of battle the preparation of the combatants often determines the outcome. Tyndale used the time at Worms between 1525 and 1527 to supply his people with Luther's secret weapon: faith. The rediscovery of this essence of Christianity, lost for twelve centuries, required a strategy for communicating it to the masses.

In addition, after the completion of the New Testament translation and printing, the Old Testament had to be translated. That required learning the Hebrew language and obtaining manuscripts and recent printings from which to translate. It was a time of learning and working to fulfill the purpose that Tyndale and the members of the Secret Society believed God had for them. At the same time, Wolsey, More and Cochlaeus were desperately seeking to cut off the supply of these forbidden books by destroying the source. As time passed, however, the truth of William Tyndale's theology took root in more and more fields ready and fertile for the seed he was planting.

In 1527 Tyndale left Worms and settled in Marburg in Hesse-Cassel, a Lutheran stronghold governed by Prince Philip, who had cast his lot with the Reformers. Prince Philip had founded a university that attracted men of learning, and Protestant refugees from England and Scotland were constantly passing through on their way to and from Wittenberg. For Tyndale, the refugees were a constant source of news from home, and they sought his advice on the crises being generated on the western front. John Frith was the closest of friends, and their time spent together was most valuable in terms of needed reassurance concerning the rightness of the cause. Until then William Tyndale had battled for survival on two fronts, against both Cardinal Wolsey and Henry VIII. But at that time the two enemies of Tyndale were at variance with each other over Henry's desire to divorce Catherine of Aragon and to marry Anne Boleyn. This dispute was the opening that Luther and Tyndale had to have, and they immediately signaled to the monarch their support for his right to rule even if the Church excommunicated him over the divorce issue.

It is impossible to overestimate the value of such a break in the coalition between King Henry and Wolsey. Henry VIII required only the unwavering support of the people to throw off the yoke of Rome, and Tyndale was the most efficient and effective means of ensuring that condition.

In 1528 William Tyndale issued two books that became the powder and shot for Henry VIII and the

Reformers. For Henry, *The Obedience Of A Christian Man* established the biblical basis for his right to rule and took away the Church's authority in matters of civil law. The general acceptance of the treatise by men such as Thomas Cranmer and Thomas Cromwell permitted a re-establishment of the ecclesiastical powers in a clean break with Rome and its home-grown puppets, Thomas More and Cardinal Wolsey. The enemy was outflanked. Henry had more than enough support to separate church from state. To his credit, he did not waver. Wolsey died of fright the night before his confrontation with Henry. More was tougher, and ultimately Henry's boyhood friend and companion would have to be executed. More had forfeited his popularity with the masses because of his singular views against William Tyndale.

The story of Henry's acquisition of Tyndale's *Obedience Of A Christian Man* is worth retelling here. A servant of Anne Boleyn gave his mistress a copy of the book, to her great delight. She read the book and talked about it to the bishop, who scolded her and confiscated it with a stern warning that she was the recipient of forbidden literature. Anne's complaint of the incident to Henry brought intolerance for the bishop's scolding and the return of the book. Henry, after reading it, declared that it was the greatest little book ever written.

Tyndale's literature had reached the bedroom of the king. The thrust of *Obedience Of A Christian Man* strengthened the king politically and spirtually. The events surrounding the violent assault on Tyndale's New Testament by More and Tunstal and the flagrant persecution of the Reformers in England by Wolsey and More lifted Tyndale's spirit of determination to continue his course. He wrote to strengthen faith, reminding his readers that those who are led through tribulation and adversity are the men and women God specially seeks to honor. Henry VIII was found at that time to be counted in that number. "If God promises life, He slayeth first; when He builds He casteth all down first. God is no patcher; He cannot build on another's foundation," recorded Tyndale in his book.

Obedience Of A Christian Man was embraced by lovers of the Reformation and those discontented with the pope. Tyndale's later condemnation of Henry's divorce alienated his new ally, but not before Henry gained the strength to break with the Church of Rome.

On March 7, 1528, Sir Thomas More was licensed by Bishop Tunstal to refute the work of Tyndale. But the truth, once established, has power to stand against any and all comers, and More, against his convictions, resorted to rage and violence, isolating himself from the growing mainstream of reform. The dialogue between More and Tyndale degenerated into name calling and, in reality, destroyed More's reputation as a champion of academic freedom and fair scholarship. It was a low point for them both.

Simultaneous with the publication of *Obedience Of A Christian Man*, William Tyndale translated Martin Luther's treatise, "Justification By Faith," an attack on the spiritual leaders "who had taken away the key of knowledge and beggared the people." Tyndale titled this translation "The Wicked Mammon" and it, too, was widely circulated.

In 1528-29 William Tyndale completed the translation of the Pentateuch from the Hebrew and sailed for Hamburg to get it printed. Over two years had been invested in the translation, and Tyndale carried with him the completed manuscripts, a work that was as extensive in itself as the New Testament. Then disaster struck. His ship was capsized by a violent storm that nearly cost Tyndale his life. The ship sank and the manuscripts were lost. William Tyndale took another ship to Hamburg where he met two other English refugees, Miles Coverdale and John Rogers. They became his disciples ("disciplined learners"), who later carried on the work of translation after Tyndale's premature martyrdom. Coverdale was a diplomat like Erasmus and was patronized by both More and Thomas Cromwell, who had assumed the post vacated by the death of Cardinal Wolsey. By 1531 the Pentateuch was completed for the second time, and the printing was undertaken at Antwerp.

The same scholarship demonstrated in the New Testament translation was evident in the Pentateuch. Tyndale discovered the Hebrew to have an even greater affinity for English rendering than the Greek. Westcott observed, "William Tyndale felt by a happy instinct the potential affinity between Hebrew and English idioms and he enriched our language and thought forever with the characteristics of the Semitic mind."

In 1531 Tyndale printed the translation of the Book of Jonah, and in the preface compared England to Nineveh, with the exception that Nineveh repented while England, especially the bishops, continued to prosecute its evil. English Church leaders intensified their passion to stop Tyndale from completing further works. He was now moving more often, as the authorities were always on his heels. Had it not been for the Secret Society, he would have been captured early on. Now the pressure was much greater to arrest the man whose forbidden literature was single-handedly destroying the Roman Church in England. Henry VIII was lost to the Church, and every passing day powerful leaders of the Church were switching their allegience to Henry's camp, apparently precipitated by the example Tyndale championed in his writings and life, not by fear of being on the losing side. This truth echoed through the centuries by virtue of their testimonies, as they, too, tasted the fire in Queen Mary's succession to the throne twenty years later.

Martin Luther zealously courted Henry and made advances for him to join the cause. Henry VIII would never make such a commitment; his commitment was to England alone. Nevertheless, the philosophy of the two sides had the same spiritual conviction at their roots. Henry actively recruited the dissidents within the Roman Church, but would never compromise the sovereignty of England as he viewed it.

Tyndale's eventual denunciation of Henry's divorce, resulting from a spiritual conviction and published in "Practice of Prelates" in 1531, precluded any hopes of his returning to England as a free man. His life was that of a nomad, travelling from place to place to avoid detection, translating and revising as he could. Finally, in exhaustion, he chose the English House at Antwerp to oversee the transport of his books to England. The house was that of Thomas Poyntz, a relative of Lady Walsh of Little Sodbury Manor. The year was 1533.

"This term, *myself*, is not in the Gospel." So spoke William Tyndale in *The Wicked Mammon*. His countenance was one of humility, but his life was one of courage and endurance. He practiced what he preached. He set aside two days a week that he referred to as his "days of pastime." Of these two days, Monday and Saturday, one day was given to visiting all the English refugees in the city and relieving their wants; the other day was used to seek out every hole and corner where he suspected any poor person was and when there was a need to relieve their wants.

Most of what we know of Tyndale personally is through his association with John Frith. Frith was brilliant, a master of language and logic concerning the Scriptures. We believe that if Tyndale were able to speak, he would insist on lifting above the sea of martyrs this one champion of faith worthy to stand beside his captain.

John Frith, who knew Tyndale's inmost mind, wrote to Sir Thomas More: "Grant that the Word of God, I mean the text of Scripture, may go abroad in our English tongue, as other nations have it in their tongue, as my brother William Tyndale and I have done; and we will promise to write no more."

Frith and Tyndale labored together as often as the young disciple was on the Continent. Frith was the eyes and ears of Tyndale in England, and may be aptly described as the brains of the English movement. His faith overcame his fear; he was the defender of truth and was as articulate in that role as Hugh Latimer had been through his years of lecturing at Cambridge.

Frith lived in Holland with his wife, whom Tyndale described as well content with the will of God. She was aware of the constant danger to which her husband submitted himself every time he secretly went into England. Intelligence-gathering is risky business, but ever so necessary to the success of the underdog.

Frith had "business" in England in 1532, and his travels took him to Reading where his haggard appearance and apparent poverty got him arrested as a vagabond. The sequel is comical: As was common in those days, the arrested vagrant was placed in stocks in the city center for bystanders to taunt and torment at their leisure until the prisoner's plight was relieved by starvation. As luck would have it, a fellow Etonian from Cambridge wandered by and looked pitifully on the poor prisoner. Frith recognized the fellow and proceeded to converse in Greek from the *Iliad*, to the total dismay of his former classmate. Straightway the fellow appealed to the authorities and influenced them to release the distinguished vagabond.

Days later the record positions Frith in London, where he was stalked by spies for Sir Thomas More, who had offered a reward for his arrest. Frith sought to escape in a disguise, but he was betrayed. The authorities seized him and imprisoned him in the Tower of London.

What transpired next is truly one of the strangest episodes in the history of the Reformation. Thomas Cranmer was the new archbishop and was sympathetic to the Reformers, especially to a man of the stature and prominence of John Frith. Cranmer attempted to orchestrate his escape and ordered two men of his charge to transport the prisoner from the Tower to the archbishop's palace at Croydon. Cranmer had given specific instructions: "If you can, do so induce the prisoner to *accommodate* his view somewhat to the beliefs of his judges. If you fail to do this, connive his escape. I will see that no punishment comes on you. I do not want John Frith burned."

An additional twist to this sequel was More's dismissal as Henry's chancellor at the time Frith was in the Tower. An archenemy was gone; however, Frith's accusers were Bishops Stokesley and Longland, veterans in persecution. Thomas Cromwell had assumed More's position. He was a well-known sympathizer of the Reformers and possibly had used Frith as an agent to mastermind the establishment of the "new" Church. This cloak-and-dagger activity is speculative, but not without certain proof as evidenced by correspondence of Cromwell's envoy, Stephen Vaughn, who sought the continental Reformers' help in making a "legal" break with the Roman Church.

Frith had been charged on the only point that would cause him to arch his back and stand fast in defense. His position on transubstantiation (the mystical conversion of wine to blood and bread to flesh) was exclusive; Tyndale had chosen not to become involved in the controversy, even though he supported Frith's view. Frith's work, "The Presence of Christ in The Lord's Supper," was a masterpiece of tact, knowledge and logic in which he stated his belief that no carnal presence was in the elements.

The Protestant church of the twentieth century differs in its views of communion as a denominational preference; however, transubstantiation has been reconciled as a distinct departure from the Catholic dogma. We owe that distinction to Frith and Wycliffe, among others. However, it was a volatile subject in 1532 and Frith would not—could not—recant his position.

In their accusations, his persecutors took advantage of this schism in the Reformist Movement to justify the burning of the supposed heretic.

Cranmer's constables, with Frith in their care, failed to get an assurance of compromise from him and worse, could not convince him to escape. Frith reckoned that he was being "called to witness" to the truth and dared not turn back. His own words concerning his position have been preserved for posterity:

> Now being taken by the highest powers, and, as it were by Almighty God's permission and providence, delivered into the hands of the Bishops, only for religion and doctrines such as in conscience, and under pain of damnation, I am bound to maintain and defend; if I should now start aside, and run away, I should run from my God, and from the testimony of His Holy Word and be worthy of a thousand hells. And therefore, I most heartily thank you both, for your goodness toward me, beseeching you to bring me where I was appointed to be brought, for else I will go hither all alone.

Cranmer tried in vain to dissuade him. Frith willingly embraced the fire, tied to the stake back to back with another young man who was being martyred with him. A glimpse of Frith's character is revealed in his correspondence to the congregation he pastored. From his cell in the Tower of London he wrote,

The burning of John Frith and Andrew Hemet.

"Doubt not that God shall so provide for you that you shall have an hundred mothers for one, an hundred homes for one, and that in this life; as I have proved by experience."

Frith was dead. Tyndale had lost his son in the faith and mourned their temporary separation, which would be ended in three more years. Tyndale continued his labors with the help of John Rogers and Miles Coverdale. Their priority was to translate the Old Testament from the Hebrew; nevertheless, his passion was to revise the New Testament so that "it would take its fullest shape."

The Last Days

Antwerp was the most important commercial city in Europe, and merchants from all over the world were given the privileges of her citizens. English mechants were afforded a nobleman's house close to the cathedral. The city was in the jurisdiction of Holy Roman Emperor Charles V, but as long as the merchants were inside their homes, they were secure from the authorities except in the cases of great crimes. But in the streets a man could be seized and transported to a place where the Church's laws against heresy could be put in force against him.

Copyright laws did not exist, and forgeries of books pirated by unscrupulous printers and profiteers were common. William Tyndale experienced such a counterfeit with George Joye, an English refugee who took the liberty of correcting Tyndale's New Testament using the Latin Vulgate. Joye printed the text with his changes and angered Tyndale with a translation that was less than faithful to the meaning of the Greek.

To compensate for this imposter, Tyndale's revised New Testament of 1534 contained a title page and a denunciation of Joye's wickedness and dishonesty. The incident had convinced Tyndale that his translations could no longer go forth anonymously. He wrote in his preface, "I neither can nor will suffer of any man that he shall go take my translation and correct it without name, and make such changing as I myself durst not do as I hope to have my part in Christ though the whole world should be given me for my labor."

By 1535 Cranmer and Cromwell had succeeded in controlling the persecution, and people could even possess an English Bible and read it. William Tyndale entertained thoughts of returning to England, as outside the safe house in Antwerp one took his life into his own hands.

Tyndale had been living in the English House for about a year when an Englishman arrived who struck up a friendship that grew closer with time. Henry Phillips flattered himself into William Tyndale's confidence and obtained guest privileges to the house under the guise of making use of Tyndale's books and study.

Thomas Poyntz, the master of the house, distrusted the fellow, but Tyndale's heart went out to him. Phillips timed his move to act when Poyntz had business

The martyrdom of Master William Tyndall in Flanders, by Vilvord Castle.

outside the city. Under the pretense of needing to borrow money because of losing his purse, Phillips set up an ambush outside the compound and, with Tyndale leading the way, signalled his henchmen to seize the translator and hurry him to the emperor's attorney. Tyndale's possessions were seized for evidence on order of the attorney, and the prisoner was quickly conveyed to the castle of Vilvorde, established as a state prison. Tyndale was confined to the dungeon of this fortress, which was constructed in the style of the Bastille in Paris.

This dungeon was the last residence of William Tyndale. No hope really ever existed for his release. He spent his last five hundred days in a cold, dark and lonely cell deep inside the castle. The only record of this time is contained in a letter written to the prison warden requesting warmer clothes, a candle and, above all, his Hebrew Bible, grammar and dictionary.

I believe, right worshipful, that you are not ignorant of what has been determined concerning me [by the Council of Brabant]; therefore I entreat your lordship and that by the Lord Jesus, that if I am to remain here [in Vilvorde] during the winter, you will request the Procureur to be kind enough to send me from my goods which he has in his possession, a warmer cap, for I suffer extremely from cold in the head, being afflicted with a perpetual catarrh, which is considerably increased in this cell. A warmer coat also, for that which I have is very thin: also a piece of cloth to patch my leggings: my overcoat is worn out; my shirts are also worn out. He has a woolen shirt of mine, if he will be kind enough to send it. I have also with him leggings of thicker cloth for putting on above; he also has warmer caps for wearing at night. I wish also his permission to have a lamp in the evening, for it is wearisome to sit alone in the dark. But above all, I entreat and beseech your clemency to be urgent with the Procureur that he may kindly permit me to have my Hebrew Bible, Hebrew Grammar, and Hebrew Dictionary, that I may spend my time with that study. And in return, may you obtain your dearest wish, provided always it be consistent with the salvation of your soul. But if, before the end of the winter, a different decision be reached concerning me, I shall be patient, abiding the will of God to the glory of the grace of my Lord Jesus Christ, whose Spirit, I pray, may ever direct your heart. Amen.

—W. Tyndale.

Cranmer and Cromwell appealed for Tyndale's release without success. Poyntz risked his life and liberty and was incarcerated himself, although he later escaped.

On October 6, 1536, William Tyndale was tied to his stake, strangled and burned. His last words were: "Lord, open the King of England's eyes."

Chapter 6

Tyndale's Influence on English

Imagine an English-speaking world denied Shakespeare, Spencer, Tennyson, Bunyan, Newton, Wesley, T.S. Eliot and C.S. Lewis. They all had one common influence, a man named William Tyndale, born in 1494, whose prose and creativity in designing our language is the most grossly overlooked contribution to western civilization in the annals of our history.

The ultimate test of a prophet in the historical, biblical panorama is for his prophecy to come to pass in the generations following. There is no single person in the annals of modern history whose words of prophecy have had the power of their truth whenever and wherever they were rediscovered and practiced as those penned by William Tyndale.

Tyndale's understanding and comprehension were embodied in the spirit of a statement he made in the dining room of Sir John Walsh at Little Sodbury Manor when he refuted a bishop who had stated that it would be better to be without God's laws than without the pope's. Remembering the Prologue to Erasmus' Greek-Latin Bible (from which he would translate and print the English New Testament), Tyndale exclaimed, "I defy the Pope and all *his* laws, and if God spare my life, I will make it possible for the boy who drives the plow to know more Scriptures than you."

With God's help Tyndale accomplished the task that realized that goal, and literally millions of men and women, with nothing more than his English translation, proved his words over and over again as the centuries unfolded.

In his translation of the Bible, Tyndale wittingly shaped the English language so a mental picture would form in the mind of the reader as he read the message of the text. At that time the masses were the victims of tyranny from the religious establishment and the state. That tyranny denied them the freedom to own, read or memorize God's Word in the vernacular, and worse, necessitated an earthly advocate for God's children to relate to their Creator.

Tyndale sought every possible expression to illuminate the message. It was the spiritual nature of man that he attempted to awaken in the reader. The apostle Paul had directed his message to the innermost man, the one that was distinguished from the physical body and soul. To know God and to experience God was in the spiritual dimension. The contest for man was not a warfare of flesh and blood, but of principalities and powers.

Tyndale's word order and cadence touched the reader's spirit, then and now, and allowed him to know and trust in whom he believed. The spiritual man cried "Daddy" to the heavenly Father in an expression of intimacy that a loving son has with a loving father, which is so reminiscent of the child-like relationship God wants. Tyndale knew that God was looking for men and women who would trust Him. In the world where principalities and powers function, it was not perfection that God sought. After all, that's why He sacrificed His perfect Son. It was trust in that sacrifice that God sought. That is the message stated and restated in the text, which Tyndale so ably portrayed with his translation. The Hebrew and the Greek pictured events; so, too, Tyndale's words recreated those pictures. (Tyndale stated that it was a thousand times easier to translate the original languages to English than to Latin, Spanish, French or German.)

The Greek manuscripts and fragments of Scripture discovered down through the centuries have revealed a remarkable common characteristic: They are in the colloquial character. That is, they are in the spoken language of the people who first received it. Tyndale must have sensed that fact because he employed that methodology—so the common man could understand. It was the context of Scripture that God wanted communicated. It is axiomatic; the *whole* is equal to the sum of its parts.

Prior to 1900, the Greek language of biblical manuscripts was thought to be the language used by first century scholars. In actuality it was the language used by ordinary people, and it communicated a thought or argument with simplicity. The world is full of people who think that sacred Scripture should be elevated above the common use. But the New Testament writers in the first century wrote, under the inspiration of God, in ordinary Greek, and William Tyndale, under the same inspiration and without the archeological evidence yet to be discovered, did the same thing.

When Tyndale was seized and incarcerated, Coverdale and Rogers continued to assist him. Even while Tyndale was in prison, they served the needed apprenticeship to give his work its full shape after his death. The proof of this effort was manifested after his execution. Coverdale was granted a license to print and distribute the whole Bible in 1536. Rogers was also granted permission to publish his Bible under the pen name of Matthews in 1537. The work was Tyndale's; the honor Coverdale's and Rogers'.

By 1539, Coverdale collaborated with the English government and by virtue of a royal injunction, the

Great Bible was published and distributed to every church in England between 1539 and 1541. But in the decade following, instability and unrest limited the freedom to print God's Word, and its printing went underground once again. During her reign, Bloody Mary (1553-1558) sought to re-establish Catholicism in England and martyred over 300 reformers.

John Knox and Myles Coverdale sought asylum on the Continent. Knox joined John Calvin in Geneva and helped publish the Geneva Bible in 1560. The Geneva Bible was a masterpiece of Reformation literature. It was the biblical text of Tyndale with thousands of explanatory notes that promoted learning and understanding of the text. The notes aroused the monarch, then Queen Elizabeth, and she approved the publishing of the Bishop's Bible in England in 1568. Again, Tyndale's text was the basis for the new Bible, but without the notes of the Geneva edition.

In 1582 the Catholic Church approved the translation of the Latin Vulgate into English. Perhaps this event, more than any other, evidenced the complete vindication of Tyndale's labor and life. Forty-six years after his execution, the Church published in English the very work that thousands of men and women had been martyred for demanding the right to possess.

The Geneva Bible continued to grow in popularity during the seventeenth century. It became the Bible of choice for Shakespeare, Spenser, the Puritans and the working classes. It was the Bible that came over on the Mayflower with the Pilgrims and was the Bible of America for over a hundred years.

However, in that same century the Geneva Bible gave way to the King James version, and Parliament commissioned Oliver Cromwell to execute the king for attempting to take away the rights gained by martyr's blood. It was during this period as well that John Bunyan and John Milton wrote the greatest and most beloved literature of England, using the prose and poetry of Tyndale's Bible.

In the eighteenth century, those words influenced the poetry of John Newton, William Cowper, Charles Wesley and Augustine Toplady. Newton and Cowper wrote "Amazing Grace" and composed the first hymn book; Charles Wesley wrote hundreds of songs that influenced millions; and Toplady, hiding under an enormous rock in a violent thunderstorm, wrote "Rock of Ages," the most beloved hymn in our language.

By 1790, William Carey, who honed his skills as a preacher by preaching to birds and animals near his little parish in Moulton, was burdened to reach those who had never heard the gospel. Thus world missions were born, and Carey boarded a ship for India to practice what he preached. This mans's burden to reach the lost with God's Word was shared in the nineteenth century by English-speaking men and women who took the gospel to virtually every nation.

The power of God's Word in English has also been manifested over the centuries in its influence on common law and democratic government, finding expression in the Bill of Rights, the Declaration of

Independence and the U.S. Constitution. Wherever the English conquered and colonized, their laws and stress on individual freedom took root and guaranteed human rights.

In America, the Bible in English was the textbook for liberty that Jonathan Edwards, George Whitefield and John Wesley so eloquently expounded and that the people imbibed for its truth and freedom. Thus the courage to rebel from Mother England was undertaken from a conviction that resistance to tyranny was obedience to God. Furthermore, the colonies never doubted that God was on their side. England never lost a battle in the Revolution, but the colonies won the war.

Until this generation, the Bible was the most popular book ever printed. Except for the printing of Mao Tse Tung's Little Red Book in 1951, each year since 1611 the Bible has been the "best seller" worldwide. In the English-speaking world, the Bible has been the best seller, without exception, for over three hundred fifty years.

That is the legacy of one man who worked alone, exiled from his beloved England, separated from friends and family, enduring bitter cold and discomfort, living in poverty and finally imprisoned and murdered for daring to obey God rather than man.

Chapter 7

Faith Rediscovered

God's Word is a book of promises (prophecy). To counterfeit those promises, the devil employed false prophets who were designed to confuse and lead the people of God astray.

God's Word demands defiance of earthly circumstance when that circumstance conflicts with His promises. Tyndale personified that message in his eleven-year exile. Shipwreck, poverty, hunger, illness, separation from family and loved ones, and death of friends were earthly circumstances that Tyndale faced every day. Yet we do not find a trace of the conflict between God's promises that Tyndale discovered in the text and the reality of his peril. Tyndale was intimately acquainted with the spiritual dimension of his earthly existence and that spiritual connection was maintained by his faith. So from the mind and pen of this man, we are lifted above the disappointments of life to a communion with God when we act on His promises.

Tyndale mastered the Scriptures, and God revealed to him His control over history, His Church, government, civilization and children by virtue of the promises that were made to those who acted on them. There were conditional and unconditional promises, and Tyndale and Luther re-discovered this essence of Christianity that the apostle Paul and the New Testament writers had faithfully recorded. But the established church denounced the simplicity of this discovery; moreover, they were unnerved by the potential it contained for undermining their control over the masses and especially the monarchs.

In Genesis God promised Christ's victory over the devil (3:15); Noah's preservation in the Ark (6:18); and Abraham's fathering a great nation (12:2-3).

These and numerous other promises that were made God faithfully brought to pass through men and women in succeeding generations who acted on those words no matter what the earthly circumstance. For example, Abraham and Sarah acted and Isaac was born in spite of the fact that Sarah was physiologically past the age of child-bearing.

God told Moses to issue conditional promises to the Israelites. In Exodus 15:26 they were promised freedom from sickness, long life, defense from enemies, safety and victory—all for obedience. The consequences for disobedience were illness, death, defeat and estrangement from God. Tyndale understood from the Old Testament record that God was looking for people throughout history who would trust Him. In order to bring the promises to pass, God entered into the affairs of man, for God was not a man to lie or the Son of man to repent. What He said, He would do. To accomplish His purpose, for His Word to go free, nations were raised up and nations were brought down.

In the New Testament the promises continued to be laid down, but in a way that embraced all of mankind and not just the Jewish element. Tyndale observed that in truth God was no respecter of persons. The good news that Paul and the New Testament writers revealed was that the obedience demonstrated by Jesus broke down the walls of the Jewish claims on God and permitted all of mankind to have access to God, not through liturgy, ceremony and the temple, but through trust, from anyone who would act on His words.

To the intellectual Greek and Roman community, this acting, called faith, was *divine madness*. Acting first on the divine proposition, that God sacrificed His only begotten Son to satisfy the universal payment for sin, ensured sinful man's access to God because Jesus defeated death, hell and the grave by the single miraculous event of His resurrection. Jesus' claims about Himself included the immaculate conception (virgin birth) and incarnation (God with flesh), as well as the resurrection. There was no further need to perform rituals, including the blood sacrifice of animals, to cover man's sin and satisfy God. Jesus' obedience and sacrifice consummated those symbolic acts in His life and death, burial and resurrection. From eternity's view, only those who looked to Jesus would gain access to Heaven.

The magnitude of Christ's claims infuriated the religious establishment. The Judean authorities violated every ordinance of their religion to silence Christ. The heresy charges they brought against Jesus Christ were repeated through the centuries by established religion, even the new religion of Christianity, whenever and wherever evil men could gain the upper hand in confining the new faith to four walls, even to creating an earthly hierarchy of false prophets that preempted the Way that Jesus had established for men to have access to God.

As the cycles of insanity revolved, it again required human sacrifice (martyrdom) to break the devil's grip on the souls of men. Looking back on the ages, the question that begs to be answered as hundreds of men and women burned at the stake is, "Where was God?" No better answer can be articulated than that given by T.S. Eliot in *Murder in the Cathedral*: "...martyrdom is no accident. A martyr is always made by the design of God for his love of men, to warn them, and to lead them back to His ways."

As for the religious establishment in Jesus' day, their fear of the truth drove them to kill Him. Their control over men was eliminated by His fulfilling the Old Testament promises concerning Himself. He was the last Lamb they would slaughter in order for the masses to have their sin debt atoned.

Jesus claimed that the human body was the temple for the Holy Spirit, not the earthly temples and synagogues. Jesus promised that wherever two or more are gathered, He would be present. The truth of Scripture has been there all the time, but it has not stopped the devil from distorting it through the instrument of false prophets. By A.D. 600, the establishment was rebuilding its earthly temples and putting God back in a box. Men were busy creating an earthly hierarchy and structuring Christianity with human laws and ordinances. Eventually, the Word that went free in the first century was restricted to one language, Latin, and its meaning was interpreted by a small band of self-serving, double-minded men who dominated western civilization. Even today dozens of denominations have their own eccentricities and their own doctrines developed from the isolated experiences of the founder.

Luther, Tyndale and the Reformers rediscovered the "priesthood of individual believers" by allowing the Word to go free in the language of the people. The proof of that truth was validated in each succeeding generation. Tyndale rightly pictured in his English the

Church as the congregation, not the cathedrals and monasteries with their begging friars, crooked bishops and vain cardinals who spent their earthly existence jockeying for position and power. So the establishment crucified Jesus in the first century and burned Tyndale and the Reformers in the fifteenth century. What price freedom?

In reality, God's Word lifts the spiritual nature of men to a communion with Himself. In that fellowship the earthly trials and tribulations become connecting rods to God that overcome the mundane tension created by tyrants. Tyndale knew by experience what an honor it was to be found worthy of the persecution the devil and the world administered. To that end, his life and labor were victories for God and His Word.

The Bible did not rise to the place it now occupies because God sent somebody with a box of tricks to prove its divine authority. Its answer to the spiritual needs of men and women made the Word what it is. Like the blacksmith's anvil that wore out a hundred hammers and still stood firm, it has outworn the attacks of ten thousand enemies. What is more significant, the Bible has lived in spite of the folly of its defenders.

Luther and Tyndale rediscovered faith, the lost message of the Church. If the story had ended with Tyndale, the message of faith would be suspect in our generation. However, history, when rightly divided, reveals an expression of the message's power in the works of those such as Shakespeare and Spenser, who plagiarized Tyndale's English Bible in their writings, thereby elevating English literature to a level of excellence, uniting a people to a love of freedom which is being realized as much today as it was in the darkest hours of the Reformation.

Tyndale acted on the promises in the good times as well as in the bad. His life was likened to Isaiah, who, twenty-two hundred years earlier, proclaimed: "Who is among you that feareth the lord, that obeyeth the voice of the servant, that walketh in darkness, and hath no light? Let him trust in the name of the Lord, and rest upon his God. Behold, all you that kindle a fire, that compass yourselves about with sparks: walk in the light of your fire and in the spark that you have kindled. This shall you have of my hand: you shall lie down in sorrow" (Is. 50:10-11).

Epilogue

The Scriptures that Fired the Hearts of the Lollards

We at Lollard House thought you would enjoy reading some passages from Tyndale's Bible. These passages encouraged and strengthened the early reformers to "love not their own lives, even unto death." These men and women were stirred to deep commitment to the person of the Lord Jesus as they read and meditated on these and other precious promises.

Tyndale's Bible released these people from serving a system of ignorance. As our early fathers were released from this bondage, they ushered in the greatest period of reformation and revival in human history.

Like Tyndale, we, too, are committed to a deep relationship with Jesus Christ, embracing these and other promises. Like the Lollards of old, we know that radically embracing Christ and His promises will usher in a twenty-first century reformation revival in the Tyndale tradition of commitment, holiness and progress into God's purposes for humanity.

Promise

(old and new version)

There he made them an ordinaūce &
a law, & there he tempted them, & sayd:
*Yf ye wyl herken vnto the voyce of ȳ
Lorde youre God, and wyll doo that
which is ᶜ right in his sight & wil geue
an eare vnto his cōmaūdementes, and
kepe all his ordinaunces: than wyll J
putte none of these dyseases vpon thee
whiche J broughte vpon the Egyptis
ans, for J am the Lorde thy surgion.

Exodus 15:26

And said, If you will hearken unto the voice of the Lord your God, and will do that which is right in his sight and will give an ear unto his commandments, and keep all his ordinances: then will I put none of these diseases upon thee which I brought upon the Egyptians, for I am the Lord thy surgeon.

Other Promises

**Modern spellings
from
Tyndale's Bible
of 1551**

Exodus 23:22

But and if thou shalt hearken unto his voice, and keep all that I shall tell thee, then I will be an enemy unto thine enemies, and an adversary unto thine adversaries.

Leviticus 18:5

Keep therefore mine ordinances, and my judgements which if a man do he shall live thereby: for I am the Lord.

Deuteronomy 16:20

But in all things follow righteousness and thou mayest live and enjoy the land which the Lord thy God gives thee.

Deuteronomy 30:2-3

And come again unto the Lord thy God, and hark unto His voice according to all that I command thee this day: both thou and thy children in all thine heart, and all thy soul.

Then the Lord thy God will turn thy captivity and have compassion upon thee and go and fetch thee again from all the nations, among which the Lord thy God shall have scattered thee.

Deuteronomy 30:16

In that I command thee this day to love the Lord thy God, and to walk in his ways, and to keep his commandments, his ordinances and his laws: that thou may live and multiply, and that the Lord thy God may bless thee in the land, whither thou goes to possess it.

Job 5:25

Thou shalt see also, that thy seed shall increase, and that thy posterity shall be as the grass upon the earth.

Psalm 1:1-3

Blessed is the man that goes not in the counsel of the ungodly: that abides not in the way of sinners, and sits not in the seat of the scornful. But delights in the law of the Lord: and exercises himself in his law, both day and night. Such a man is like a tree planted by the waterside, that brings forth his fruit in due season.

His leaves shall not fall off, and like whatever he does, it shall prosper.

Psalm 5:12

For thou Lord gives thy blessing unto the righteous: and with thy favorable kindness thou defends him, as with a shield.

Psalm 15:1-5

Lord, who shall dwell in thy tabernacle, who shall rest upon thy holy hill.

Even he that leads an uncorrupt life: that does the thing which is right, and that speaks the truth from his heart.

He that uses no deceit in his tongue: he that does no evil to his neighbor, and slanders not his neighbors.

He that sits not by the ungodly, but makes much of they that fear the Lord: he that swears unto his neighbor, and disappoints him not.

He that giveth not his money up on usury, and takes no reward against the innocent.

Who so does these things, shall never be removed.

Psalm 27:14

Tarry thou the Lord's leisure, be strong, let

thine heart be of good comfort, and wait thou for the Lord.

Psalm 37:4

Delight thou in the Lord, and he shall give thee thy heart's desire.

Psalm 37:5-6

Commit thy way unto the Lord, set thy hope in him, and he shall bring it to pass.

He shall make thy righteousness as clear as the light, and thy just dealing as the noon day.

Psalm 50:23

Who so offers me thanks and praise, he honors me: and this is the way, whereby I will show him the saving health of God.

Psalm 91:14

Because he has set his love upon me, I shall deliver him: I shall defend him, for he has known my name.

Proverbs 3:5-6

Put thy trust in the Lord with all thine heart: and lean not unto thine own understanding. In all thy ways have respect unto him, and he shall order thy goings.

Proverbs 3:7-8

Be not wise in thine own conceit but fear the Lord, and depart from evil: so shall thy navel be whole, and thy bones strong.

Proverbs 13:18

He that thinks scorn to be reforms, comes to poverty and shame: but who so receives correction, shall come to honor.

Isaiah 2:2-4

It will be also in process of time: that the hill where the house of the Lord is built, shall be the chief among hills, and exalted above all little hills. And all the heathen shall stream unto him, and the multitude of people shall go unto him, speaking thus one to another: up, let us go to the hill of the Lord, and to the house of the God of Jacob: that he may show us his way, and that we may walk in his paths. For the law shall come out of Zion, and the word of God from Jerusalem, and that countenance amongst the heathen, and shall reform the multitude of people: So that they shall break their swords and spears, to make scythes, sickles and saws thereof. From that time forth shall not one people lift up weapons against another, neither shall they learn to fight from thence forth.

Isaiah 7:14

And therefore the Lord shall give you a to-ken of himself: Behold, a virgin shall conceive and bear a son, and shall call his name Emmanuel.

Isaiah 40:31

But unto them that have the Lord before their eyes, shall strength be increased, eagles wings shall grow upon them: when they run, they shall not fall: and when they go, they shall not be weary.

Isaiah 44:3

For I shall pour water upon the dry ground rivers upon the thirsty. I shall pour my spirit upon the seed and mine increase upon the flock.

Isaiah 54:2

Make thy tent wider and spread out the hanging of thy habitat: spare not, lay forth thy coat and make fast thy stakes:

Isaiah 60:1-22

And therefore get thee up by times, for thy light comes, and the glory of the Lord shall rise up upon the fore lo, while the darkness and cloud cover the earth and all the people, the Lord shall show the light and his glory shall be seen in thee. The Gentiles shall come to thy light, and kings to the brightness that springs forth upon thee. Lift up thine eyes, and look round about thee: All these gather themselves, and come to thee. Sons shall come unto thee from far, and daughters shall gather themselves to thee on every side. When thou see this, thou shalt marvel exceedingly, and thine heart shall be opened when the power of the sea shall be converted unto thee (that is) when the strength of the Gentiles shall come unto thee. The multitude of camels shall cover thee, the dromedaries of Midian and Ephah. All they of Sheba shall come, bringing gold and incense, and showing the praise of the Lord. All the cattle of Kedar shall be gathered unto thee, the rams of Nebaioth shall serve thee, to be offered unto mine altar, which I have chosen, and in the house of my glory which I have garnished. But what are these that lie here like the clouds, and as the doves flying to their windows. The Isles also shall gather them unto me, and specially the ships of the sea: that they may bring the sons far, and their silver and their gold with them, unto the name of the Lord thy

God, unto the holy one of Israel, that has glorified thee: Strangers that build up thy walls, and thy kings shall do thy service. For when I am angry, I smite thee: and when it pleases me, I pardon thee. Thy gates shall stand open still both day and night, and never be shut: that the host of the Gentiles may come, and that their kings may be brought unto thee. For every people and kingdom that serve not thee, shall perish, and be destroyed with the sword. The glory of Lebanon shall come unto thee: The fir trees, boxes, and cedars together, to garnish the place of my Sanctuary, for I will glorify the place of my feet.

Moreover those shall come kneeling unto thee, that have vexed thee: and all they that despised thee, shall fall down at thy foot. Thou shalt be called the city of the Lord, the holy Zion of Israel. Because thou has been forsaken and hated, so that no man went through thee: I will make thee glorious for ever and ever, and joyful throughout all posterities. Thou shalt suck the milk of the Gentiles, and kings breasts shall feed thee. And thou shalt know that I the Lord am thy Saviour and defender, the mighty one of Jacob. For brass will I give thee gold, and for iron silver: for wood brass, and for stones iron. I will make peace thy ruler, and righteousness thine officer. Violence and robbery shall never be heard of in thy land, neither harm and destruction within thy borders. Thy walls shall be called health, and thy gates "thee" praise God. The Sun shall never be thy daylight, and the light of the Moon shall never shine unto thee: but the Lord himself shall be thine everlasting light, and thy God shall be thy glory.

Thy Sun shall never go down, and thy Moon shall not be taken away, for the Lord himself shall be thy everlasting light, and thy sorrowful days shall be rewarded thee. Thy people shall be all godly, and possess thy land for ever: the flower of my planting, the work of my hands, whereof I will rejoice. The youngest and least shall grow in to a thousand, and the simplest into a strong people. I the Lord shall surely bring this thing to pass in his time.

Isaiah 55:7

Let the ungodly man forsake his ways and the unrighteous his imagination, and turn again unto the Lord: so shall he be merciful unto him: and to our God, for he is ready to forgive.

Isaiah 57:15

For thus says the high and excellent, even he that dwells in everlastingness, whose name is the holy one: I dwell high above and in the sanctuary, and with him also, that is of a contrite and humble spirit: that I may heal a troubled mind, and a contrite heart.

Jeremiah 17:7-8

And blessed is the man that puts his trust in the Lord, and whose hope is the Lord himself. For he shall be as a tree, that is planted by the waterside: which spreads out the root unto moistness, who the heat can not harm, when it comes, but his leaves are green. And though there grow but little fruit because of drought, yet is he not careful, but he never leaves off to bring forth fruit.

Jeremiah 23:5,6; 33:15-17

Behold, the time comes, says the Lord, that I will raise up the righteous branch of David, which shall here rule, and discuss matters with wisdom, and shall set up equity and righteousness again in the earth.

In his time shall Judah be saved, and Israel shall dwell without fear. And this is the name that they shall call him: even the Lord our righteous maker.

Jeremiah 33:15-17

In those days shall Judah be helped, and Jerusalem shall dwell safe, and he that shall call her is even GOD our righteous maker. For thus the Lord promised: David shall never want one, to sit upon the stool of the house of Israel.

Jeremiah 31:31-33

Behold, the days come (says the Lord) that I will make a new covenant with the house of Israel and with the house of Judah: not after the covenant that I made with their fathers, when I took them by the hand, and let them out of the land of Egypt: which covenant they brake, wherefore I punished them for, says the Lord: But this shall be the covenant that I will make with the house of Israel after those days, says the Lord: I will plant my law in the inward parts of them, and write it in their hearts, and will be their God, and they shall be my people.

Ezekiel 11:19-20

And I will give you one heart, and I will plant you a new spirit within your bowels. That stony heart will I take out of your body, and give you a fleshly heart: That ye may walk in my commandments, and keep mine ordinances, and do them: That ye may be my people, and I your God.

Ezekiel 36:26-27

A new heart also will I give you, and a new spirit will I put in to you: As for that stony heart I will take it out of your body, and give you a fleshly heart. I will give my spirit among you, and cause you to walk in my commandments, to keep my laws, and to fulfil them.

Joel 2:12-13

Now therefore says the Lord, Turn you unto me with all your hearts, with fasting, weeping and mourning, rent your hearts, and not your clothes. Turn you unto the Lord your God, for he is gracious and merciful, long suffering and of great compassion and ready to pardon wickedness.

Joel 2:28-29

After this, will I pour out my spirit upon all flesh: and your sons and your daughters shall prophesy: your old men shall dream dreams, and your young men shall see visions, yea, in those days I will pour out my spirit upon servants and maidens.

Matthew 5:3

Blessed are the poor in spirit, for theirs is the kingdom of heaven.

Matthew 5:4

Blessed are they that mourn: for they shall be comforted.

Matthew 5:5

Blessed are the meek: for they shall inherit the earth.

Matthew 5:6

Blessed are they which hunger and thirst for righteousness: for they shall be filled.

Matthew 5:7

Blessed are the merciful: for they shall obtain mercy.

Matthew 5:8

Blessed are the pure in heart: for they shall see God.

Matthew 5:9

Blessed are the peacemakers: for they shall be called the children of God.

Matthew 5:10-12

Blessed are they which suffer persecution for righteousness sake: for theirs is the kingdom of heaven. Blessed are ye when men revile you, and persecute you, and shall falsely say all manner of evil sayings against you for my sake. Rejoice and be glad, for great is your reward in heaven. For so persecuted they the prophets which were before your days.

Matthew 6:14

For and if ye that forgive other men their trespasses, your heavenly father shall also forgive you.

Matthew 10:39

He that finds his life, shall lose it: and he that loses his life for my sake, shall find it.

Matthew 11:28

Come unto me all ye that labor and are laden and I will ease you.

Matthew 18:20

For where two or three are gathered together in my name, there am I in the midst of them.

Matthew 19:29

And whosoever forsakes houses, or brethren, or sisters, or their father, or mother, or wife, or children, or lands, for my names sake, the same shall receive an hundred fold, and shall inherit everlasting life.

Matthew 23:12

But whosoever exalts himself, shall be brought low. And he that humbles himself, shall be exalted.

Matthew 28:20

Teaching them to observe all things, whatsoever I commanded you. And lo, I am with you always, even until the end of the world.

John 6:37

All that the father gives me, shall come to me: And him that comes unto me, I cast not away.

John 7:17

If any man will do his will, he shall know of the doctrine, whether it be of God, or whether I speak of myself.

John 7:38

He that believes on me, as says the Scripture, out of his belly shall flow rivers of water of life.

John 8:31-32

Then said Jesus to those Jews which believed on him. If ye

continue in my words, then are ye my very disciples, and shall know the truth: and the truth shall make you free.

John 10:27-30

As I said unto you: my sheep hear my voice, and I know them, and they follow me, and I give unto them eternal life, and they shall never perish, neither shall any man pluck them out of my hand. My father which gave them me, is greater than all, and no man is able to take them out of my father's hand. And I and my father are one.

John 14:13,14

And whatsoever ye ask in my name, that will I do, that the father might be glorified by the son. If ye shall ask anything in my name, I will do it.

John 14:23

Jesus answered and said unto him: if a man love me and will keep my sayings, my father also will love him, and we will come unto him, and will dwell with him.

John 16:13

How be it when he is come (I mean the Spirit of Truth) he will lead you into all truth. He shall not speak of himself: but whosoever he shall hear, that shall he speak, and he will show you things to come.

Acts 10:43

To him give all the prophets witness, that through his name, all that believe in him, shall receive remission of sins.

Romans 6:14

Let not sin have power over you. For ye

are not under the law, but under grace.

Romans 8:38-39

Yea and I am sure that neither death, neither life, neither Angels, nor rule, neither power, neither things present, neither things to come, neither high, neither low, neither any other creature shall be able to separate us from the love of God, showed in Christ Jesus our Lord.

Romans 16:19-20

For your obedience extends to all men. I am glad no doubt of you. But yet I would have you wise unto that which is good, and to be innocents as concerning evil. The God of peace tread satan under your feet shortly. The grace of our Lord Jesus Christ be with you.

I Corinthians 1:8

And wait for the appearing of our Lord Jesus Christ, which shall strengthen you unto the end, that ye may be blameless in the day of our Lord Jesus Christ.

II Corinthians 9:6

This yet remember, how that he which sows little, shall reap little, and he that sows plenty shall reap plenty.

Galatians 6:8

He that sows in his flesh, shall of the flesh reap corruption. But he that sows in the spirit, shall of the spirit reap life everlasting.

Philippians 3:21

...even the Lord Jesus Christ, which shall change our vile bodies that they may be fashioned like unto his glorious body, according to the working, whereby he is able to subdue all things unto himself.

Philippians 4:19

My God fulfill all your needs through his glorious riches in Jesus Christ.

Colossians 3:4

When Christ, which is our life, shall show himself, then shall ye also appear with him in glory.

I Timothy 4:16

Take heed unto thyself and unto learning, and continue therein. For if thou shall so do, thou shall save thyself and them that hear thee.

I John 1:9

If we knowledge our sins, he is faithful and just, to forgive us our sins, and to cleanse us from all unrighteousness.

I John 3:2

Dearly beloved, now are we the sons of God, and yet it does not appear what we shall be. But we know that when it shall appear, we shall be like him. For we shall see him as he is.

Hebrews 13:5

Let your conversation be without covetousness and be content with that ye have already. For he boldly said, I will not fail thee, neither forsake thee.

James 1:5

If any of you lack wisdom, let him ask of God which gives to all men indifferently, and casts no man in the teeth: and it shall be given him.

James 4:7

Submit yourself to God, and resist the devil, and he will flee from you.

James 4:8

Draw nigh to God, and he will draw nigh to you. Cleanse you hands ye sinners, and purge your hearts ye wavering minded.

James 4:10

Cast down yourself before the Lord and he shall lift you up.

Revelation 3:20

Behold I stand at the door and knock. If any man hear my voice and open the door, I will come in unto him, and will sup with him, and he with me.

Revelation 21:6

And he said unto me: it is done, I am Alpha and Omega, the beginning and the end, I will give to him that is athirst of the well of the water of life free.

Revelation 21:7

He that overcomes, shall inherit all things, and I will be his God, and he shall be my son.

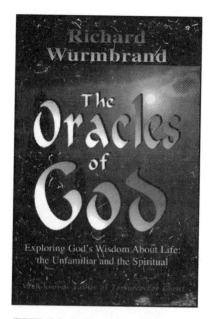

THE ORACLES OF GOD
by Richard Wurmbrand.
Richard Wurmbrand survived the torture and pain of solitary confinement in Soviet prisons and emerged to devote many years to ministering around the world. In *The Oracles of God* this older, battle-scarred pastor passes on his hard-won wisdom to a younger generation.
TPB-196p.
ISBN 1-56043-143-1
Retail $8.99

THREADS OF TIME
by Jean Swengel.
This story of divine grace traces
Protestant history from the Reformation of the sixteenth century to the present. The Christian
legacy of Ulrich Zwingli braced
many of America's forefathers
during the struggle for civil and
religious freedom. Even today it
still provides the bridge of spiritual security in these perilous
times. Includes more than 500
names in the genealogy lists!
TPB-266p.
ISBN 1-56043-776-6
Retail $8.99

HINDS' FEET ON HIGH PLACES
by Hannah Hurnard.

This illustrated version of the timeless classic was arranged by Dian Layton and beautifully illustrated by JoAnn Edington. It tells the story of Much-Afraid and her journey to the High Places with the Shepherd. Filled with exciting adventure and a triumphant conclusion, this story will teach your child the importance of following the Shepherd.
HB-128p.
ISBN 1-56043-111-3
Retail $14.99 (7⁷/₈" X 9¹/₄")

HINDS' FEET ON HIGH PLACES
by Hannah Hurnard.
A devotional for women, this book includes the entire text of the classic allegory as well as tender devotions written by Darien B. Cooper. Each devotion is so placed and prepared to bring the story's principles to life in each reader, and to draw the reader closer to her Shepherd in a personal, living relationship.

HB-336p.
ISBN 1-56043-116-4
Retail $14.99 (6" X 9")

To order toll free call:
Destiny Image
1-800-722-6774

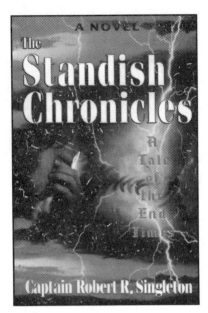

THE STANDISH CHRONICLES
by Capt. Robert R. Singleton.
When the skipper of a fishing trawler stumbles across secret documents after a freak storm, a hidden world of intrigue and evil spiritual activity forever changes life in Standish Harbor...
TPB-154p.
ISBN 1-56043-107-5
Retail $8.99

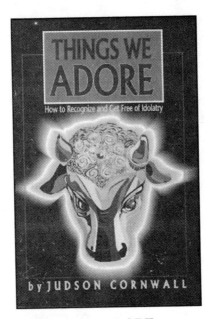

THINGS WE ADORE
by Judson Cornwall.
This book searches out the roots
of idolatry in the Old Testament,
and lays it alongside that of the
modern Church. From doctrines
of demons to the idols of men in
high places, the things we adore
have become the greatest threat
to our relationship with the Lord.
TPB-224p.
ISBN 1-56043-048-6
Retail $8.99

HOW TO REACH THE LOST GENERATION

by Brian Thomson.

Everyone wants to save this country, but few realize that the rescue of a nation begins with her children. In this book, you will find real solutions to the real problems that face kids every day on the streets of every town in the country. You can turn a bored youth group into a dynamic radical force for the Lord in your community.
TPB-196p.
ISBN 1-56043-132-6
Retail $8.99

HOW TO RAISE CHILDREN OF DESTINY

by Dr. Patricia Morgan.

This ground-breaking book high-lights the intricate link between the rise of young prophets, priests, and kings in the Body of Christ as national leaders and deliverers, and the salvation of a generation.
TPB-210p.
ISBN 1-56043-134-2
Retail $8.99

To order toll free call:
Destiny Image
1-800-722-6774

MOMMY, WHY ARE PEOPLE DIFFERENT COLORS?

by Barbara Knoll.

Carlos, Jamal, and Matt couldn't decide which color to paint their go-cart. So they decided to paint it all different colors—a rainbow racer! Through it all the three friends realize how and why God made people different colors.

TPB-24p. ISBN 1-56043-156-3
Retail $2.99 (8" X 9¼")

DADDY, DOES GOD TAKE A VACATION?

by Galen C. Burkholder.

Grown-ups take vacations to spend time together as families and to take a rest from their jobs. But as Bethany and Timmy got ready for their vacation with Mommy and Daddy, they wanted to know if God took a vacation. Here children are reassured that God is always ready to hear them and help them.

TPB-24p. ISBN 1-56043-153-9
Retail $2.99 (8" X 9¼")

MOMMY, WAS SANTA CLAUS BORN ON CHRISTMAS TOO?

by Barbara Knoll.

As Rachel and Mommy baked Christmas cookies, Rachel wanted to know how Santa Claus fit into the Christmas story. Here her mommy tells the history of Saint Nicholas and how he became Santa Claus.

TPB-24p. ISBN 1-56043-158-X
Retail $2.99 (8" X 9¼")

DADDY, ARE YOU SANTA CLAUS?

by Galen C. Burkholder.

Matthew, Trisha, and David all helped Mommy and Daddy decorate their Christmas tree. That made them think of presents—and how they got them. Here Daddy successfully answers their questions without losing his cookies and milk on Christmas Eve!

TPB-24p. ISBN 1-56043-159-8
Retail $2.99 (8" X 9¼")

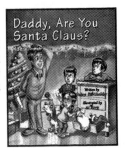